THE LORD WILL PROVIDE

Dr. Lucius M. Dalton

authorHOUSE®

AuthorHouse™
1663 Liberty Drive
Bloomington, IN 47403
www.authorhouse.com
Phone: 1-800-839-8640

First published by AuthorHouse 2/23/2011

ISBN: 978-1-4567-3703-0 (e)
ISBN: 978-1-4567-3722-1 (hc)
ISBN: 978-1-4567-3721-4 (sc)

Library of Congress Control Number: 2011902517

Printed in the United States of America

Any people depicted in stock imagery provided by Thinkstock are models, and such images are being used for illustrative purposes only. Certain stock imagery © Thinkstock.

This book is printed on acid-free paper.

In October 2009, the Holy Spirit placed upon my heart a sermon series that traced the steps of Abraham from the time the Lord called him to leave home for a land that the Lord would show him (Genesis 12:1) to the time he proved his willingness to sacrifice Isaac on Mount Moriah (Genesis 22:1-14). This series would be done in 2010 to commemorate the 125th Anniversary of Mount Moriah Baptist Church.

When the twenty-six founders of this Church met in 1885 in the home of Brother Sampson Thomas at 1220 Second Street, SW, Washington, they "believed that they were to be offered for service and sacrifice." Our church profile says, "In a biblical sense, the founders likened themselves to Abraham, whom God tempted." Since then, Genesis 22:1-14 has been the motto text of our church.

I concluded this seven-week series on October 17, 2010, the day on which we began our 125th Anniversary celebration. Those seven sermons are included in this book.

This was, in fact, one of the most difficult yet rewarding sermon series I have preached. I struggled with the text while dealing with one of the most difficult moments in my personal life. Yet, the Lord provided, and once again God showed me that nothing is too hard for God.

I want to thank the Mount Moriah Baptist Church family for giving me the opportunity to practice my preaching gift from Sunday to Sunday. I also want to thank my wife, Janice Dalton, who is my most faithful supporter; my father, Milton Dalton, and my mother, Mary Dalton, for helping us through such a difficult moment; Dr. Glenda Glover, Esq. for being counsel and advisor; to my Pastor, Dr. A.C.D. Vaughn, who told me years ago not to be afraid to publish what I had written; to Mr. Glen Burkins, who served as editor; the late Dr. R. Clinton Washington, whose love and dedication to ministry I will never forget; my executive assistant, Minister Josette Elliott, and to the spirit that keeps me grounded and on track.

To God be the Glory!
Because of Christ,
Lucius M. Dalton

This book is dedicated to Zachary and Jacob, my sons; and Troy Jr. and Timothy, my nephews……

Remember "The Lord Will Provide!" and "There is nothing too hard for the Lord!"

Table of Contents

The Trial of Faith

Genesis 12:1-9 NIV

[1]The LORD had said to Abram, "Leave your country, your people and your father's household and go to the land I will show you. [2]"I will make you into a great nation and I will bless you; I will make your name great, and you will be a blessing. [3]I will bless those who bless you, and whoever curses you I will curse; and all peoples on earth will be blessed through you." [4]So Abram left, as the LORD had told him; and Lot went with him. Abram was seventy-five years old when he set out from Haran. [5]He took his wife Sarai, his nephew Lot, all the possessions they had accumulated and the people they had acquired in Haran, and they set out for the land of Canaan, and they arrived there. [6]Abram traveled through the land as far as the site of the great tree of Moreh at Shechem. At that time the Canaanites were in the land. [7]The LORD appeared to Abram and said, "To your offspring I will give this land." So he built an altar there to the LORD, who had appeared to him. [8]From there he went on toward the hills east of Bethel and pitched his tent, with Bethel on the west and Ai on the east. There he built an altar to the LORD and called on the name of the LORD. [9]Then Abram set out and continued toward the Negev.

Genesis 11:30 says, "Now Sarai was barren; she had no children." Here we have an announcement that will affect the rest of Genesis and, in many respects, still affects our world today.

In Genesis Chapters 10-11, we have the genealogies of the Shem, Ham, and Japheth (post flood) all the way to Abram and Sarai. We see the descendants of the Japhethites (Jaf'luh-tit), the Hamites (Ham'it), and the Semites. These are the clans of Noah's sons and their lines of descendants within the nations. It is from Noah's three sons that the nations spread out over the earth after the flood.

We see in Chapter 11 where all the peoples of the earth spoke one language. In this one language, they decided to build themselves a city, with a tower that reached the heavens so that they could make a name for themselves and not be scattered over the face of the earth.

The Lord came down to see the city and the tower that the men were building. The Lord said, "If as one people speaking the same language they have begun to do this, then nothing they plan to do will be impossible for them. Come, let us go down and confuse their languages so they will not understand each other."

The Lord scattered them all over the earth. They stopped building the city, and the place was called Babel because the Lord confused their language. From there the Lord scattered people all over the earth. And the earth continued to populate.

The Bible now gives the account of Shem. Shem at age 100 became the father of Arphaxad (ahr-fak'sad), and the next 400 years of his life Shem had other sons and daughters. Arphaxad became the father of Shelah (luh) at thirty, and for the next 368 years of his life he had other sons and daughters. Shelah at age thirty had Eber, and for the next 373 years Sheluh had other sons and daughters. When Eber was thirty-four, he became the father of Peleg (pee'lig). Eber lives 396 more years, having other sons and daughters. Peleg lives thirty years and became the father of Reu (ree'yoo), and for next 179 years Pelig had other sons and daughters. Reu at the age of thirty-two became the father of Serug (sihr'uhg). He lives 175 more years, and he had other sons and daughters. Serug was thirty when he became the father of Nahor. Serug lived 170 more years, and he had other sons and daughters. When Nahor was twenty-nine years old, he became the father of Terah (ter'uh). After this he lived ninety more years and had others sons and daughters. When Terah was seventy he gave birth to Abram and later Nahor and Haran. Haran became the father of Lot. Haran dies. Abram and Nahor had wives. For the first time in this genealogy are the names of women listed. Nahor's wife was Milcah, and she gave birth, but the text says, "Now Sarai was barren; she had no children."

The genealogy ends with barrenness. It is a cryptic and descriptive ending. "Sarai was barren. She had no children." Nothing is said of the cause of her barrenness. Nothing is said about a punishment or a crime. It simply states, "Now Sarai was barren; she had no children." It seems as if the family of Genesis has come to an end. There is no future. Abram and Sarai have no potential to have children.

Yet, in Chapter 12, God (Yahweh) begins to speak. God says to Abram, "Leave your country, your people and your father's household and go to the land I will show you. I will make you into a great nation and I will bless you." God speaks directly into this situation of barrenness.

As we enter our journey this Sunday and over the next five Sundays in a series entitled, "The Lord will provide," we will see that God does have a future for the family in Genesis. There is good news. Abram and Sarai will have a child. However, this journey from barrenness to childbirth begins with the faith of Abram.

Barrenness is the condition of much of humanity today. There are many today who are empty and desolate. There are many today

4

who have no hope, no expectations, and no desires. There are persons today who, for some reason or another, are having problems looking into the future. They have nothing to look forward to. No dreams! No aspirations! No plans! They yearn for nothing!

They see their lives as sterile! Infertile! Unproductive! Unfruitful and unrewarding!! They think that God does not care! God is not listening, they say!

Maybe you feel this way today! The Good News is that Genesis does not end at Chapter 11, verse. God does speak to us during our times of barrenness. Right now God is speaking into your life. You are not without potential. God wants to begin you anew. If you have faith, God will turn your barrenness into a great future. There is hope. God has words of promise, words of summons and words of assurance. God wants to remove the barrenness from your life. God wants to turn your barrenness into life.

God is calling you by name. "Abram! Abram!" And if you respond faithfully to God's call, your barrenness will turn into birth. Your infertility will turn into fruitfulness and your poverty into surplus. The Lord will provide! But you have to respond faithfully to God's call.

First, the text suggests to us that faith requires that we leave the familiar and move into the unfamiliar. The Lord says to Abram in verse 1, "Leave your country, your people and your father's household and go to the land I will show you." Abram leaves his country, people and father's household for a land that God will show him, because verse 4 says, "So Abram left, as the Lord had told him; and Lot went with him. Abram was seventy-five years old when he set out from Haran."

Notice that the Lord tells Abram to leave. God tells Abram to leave in an order or level of increasing intimacy: his land (country), his people or kindred, and his father's house. Then the Lord gives Abram a vague goal—"to a land I will show you."

It may not be hard to leave his country. It may be a littler harder to leave his relatives. Yet, it is even more difficult to leave his father and his home. Abram is told to leave everything and head toward a land that God will show him.

Observe that the Lord has not told Abram where he is going. He does not tell him where he will end up. The Lord does not tell him anything about the land. All God says to Abram is, "Leave your country, your people, and your father's household and go to the land I will show you."

Abram is obedient. He leaves everything behind, and he heads out to an unknown destination. He leaves the familiar, and in his old age (seventy-five years old) he heads to a place that God is going to show him.

God does not tell him where he will go. God does not tell him how long it will take him to get there. God does not tell him whom he will meet along the way. God does not tell him if it is going to be an easy or difficult journey. God simply tells Abram, "leave and go." And Abram responds.

He departs from his world of presumed norms and security. His family. His friends. His familiar surroundings. His favorite market. His favorite hunting place. He basically closes his eyes and he goes. He abandons that which is familiar to him and he goes. He lets go of that which is familiar and he goes. He relinquishes that which is closest and dearest to him and he goes on a journey the ends of which he cannot predict.

What a testament of faith. Do you have this type of faith?

If God told you to pick up everything—family, clothes, car—and leave behind home, mama, daddy, friends, the familiar and go to a land that God will show you, would you go or would you stay? What would you do? If God told you to pick up everything and start on a journey to a land that you know not, would you move or would stay where you are? How many of you have the type of faith that Abram had? How many of us would leave the familiar and head toward the unfamiliar? If God told you to set out on an unknown journey, I'm wondering how many of us would set out on that journey?

Whether you would or would not is a statement of your faith. It takes a tremendous amount of faith to move from the familiar to the unfamiliar. Yet, the reality is that this is how God works.

So many of us say that we have faith, but when it comes to putting our faith into practice, we oftentimes fall short. When it comes to faith, God does tell us to leave the familiar and go toward the unfamiliar. God does this to position us for the blessing that God wants to place in our lives. And we cannot receive the blessing if we stay where we are. So God requires us to move from the familiar to the unfamiliar to position us for the blessing that God wants us to have.

If we don't get anything else out of this sermon, I hope we get this: Faith requires leaving the familiar for the unfamiliar. Sometimes we have to leave family. Sometimes we have to leave mother and father. Sometimes we have to leave friends and acquaintances. Sometimes we have to leave homes and possessions. Sometimes we have to leave favorite places. Sometimes we have to leave jobs. Sometimes we have to leave the city. Sometimes we have to leave the country. Sometimes we have to leave the normal activities of our lives and we have to step out on faith. Sometimes we have to go to an unfamiliar land.

Someplace we know not. Someplace we've never been. Someplace unclear and uncertain to us. Someplace we can't see with the naked eye. Someplace where we don't know where we will end up. Someplace where we don't know anyone. Someplace that's strange to us. Someplace we know little about. Someplace where no one knows us. Someplace that may be large or small, easy or hard. Someplace where there is only God and us we. Someplace that requires faith.

The direction from God may be vague, but we must be obedient, even under such conditions, because faith many times means moving from the familiar to the unfamiliar.

Secondly, faith is always coupled with a promise from God. The Lord says to Abram in verses 2-3, "I will make you into a great nation and I will bless you; I will make your name great, and you will be a blessing. I will bless those who bless you, and whoever curses you I will curse and all people on earth will be blessed through you."

Up until now, Abram and Sarai have heard nothing of descendants. Sarai is barren. Sarai could not have children, and this caused much sorrow in her life because a woman having a child was considered a blessing from God as well as the perfect signature of womanhood. At her age, I'm sure she had given up hope of having a child.

But God tells Abram to leave. Abram does not know where. All God says is, "...a land that I will show you." But God gives Abram a promise. The promise of God is presented in five, first-person statements: God says, "I will make you into a great nation." God says, "I will bless you." God says, "I will make your name great." God says, "I will bless those who bless you." God says, "I will curse those who curse you." Abram's obedience will allow God to bless him and, in return, it is through Abram that many nations will be blessed.

God is the One who is the giver of the gift. The gift is the blessing. Abram will be blessed with offspring. He will be blessed with well-being. He will be blessed with security. He will be blessed with prosperity. And he will be blessed with prominence.

Barrenness will no longer be in his life. Hopelessness will no longer be. Because of the faithfulness of Abram, the Lord will bless him, his wife and his descendants in ways they would not in any other way be blessed. God will eliminate their barrenness, all because Abram is willing to leave the familiar for the unfamiliar.

Your obedience, or your lack of obedience, will affect your blessings. Not only this, but your obedience, or your lack of obedience, will affect future generations.

So the question becomes: Do you really want God to rid you of the barrenness in your life? The reality is that some of us do and some of us don't. Some of us count the cost too great because it means us leaving the familiar for the unfamiliar. Some of us don't want to leave the familiar, so we just settle for the barrenness of life. Nonetheless, to move from barrenness to fertility you must leave the familiar for the unfamiliar. Where are you? Are you settling for barrenness, or do you want fertility in your life?

God does not want us to be barren. God wants us to be fertile. God does not want us to be unproductive. God wants us to be fruitful. God does not want us to be waterless. God wants us to water the earth so that it might be fruitful and multiply.

God does not want us to be barren. If you remain barren, it's not God's fault. It's your fault because you do not have enough faith to move from the familiar to the unfamiliar. Nonetheless, the calm assurance is that God leaves us with a blessing every time God tells us to step out on faith. If God tells us to step out on faith, God has attached a blessing to it.

"Go and make disciples of all nations, baptizing them in the name of the Father and of the Son and of the Holy Spirit, teaching them everything I have commanded you." What happens when you go? Jesus said, "And surely, I will be with you always, to the very end of the age." Jesus said, "Give." The promise: "And it will be given unto you. A good measure, pressed down, shaken together and running over, will be poured into your lap." Jesus said, "Ask." The promise: "And it shall be given you." "Seek." The promise: "And ye shall find." "Knock." The promise: "And it shall be opened." God never requires us to exercise our faith without a promise to bless us.

One thing I do know and that is if you step out on faith, God will bless you. If you step out on faith, God will bless you in ways you never thought our imagined. If you step out on faith, God will open the windows of heaven and pour out a blessing in your life. God, faith and blessings go hand in hand. When we step out on faith, God blesses us.

We will be blessed. Children-blessed! Spouses and significant others-blessed! Blessed in our coming and our goings. Blessed on our jobs. Blessed in our homes. Blessed in our finances. Blessed in our goals. Blessed in our objectives. Blessed with security. Blessed with strength. Blessed with well-being. Blessed with health. Blessed with prosperity. Blessed with success. Blessed with affluence.

That's Good News. The Good News is that whenever you and I step out into unfamiliar territory, there is a blessing waiting for us. I don't know what it is. I don't know when or how it will take place. I don't know what avenue it's located on. I don't even know when it will come. All I do know is that if I step out on faith, there is a blessing with my name on it. I know that if I am obedient to God, the Lord will bless me with a blessing I would have never otherwise received. God blesses us when we step out on faith.

Next, the text suggests that there will be opponents when we move from the familiar to the unfamiliar. Abram does as the Lord commands. The text says in verses 5-6, "He took his wife Sarai, his nephew Lot, all the possession they had accumulated and the people they had acquired in Haran, and they set out for the land of Canaan and they arrived there. Abram traveled through the land as far as the site of the great tree of Moreh at Shechem. At that time the Canaanites were in the land."

One half of the goal of God has been reached because Abram is obedient. He has entered the promise land. Yet, he has not possessed it as God says his ancestor's will. Abram's initial entry into the land is faced with the reality of the Canaanites. When Abram entered the land that God has promised him, there were inhabitants in that land called the Canaanites. God's promise to Abram is taken to a higher degree when he is met with the Canaanites, because the word "Canaanites" means "those who do not believe the promise."

These very same Canaanites will cause the Israelites problems all the way to the point where they actually occupy the land under the leadership of Joshua.

I won't belabor this point too long, but the fact of the matter is that when we leave the familiar for the unfamiliar, we are going to meet some Canaanites along the way. In other words, there will be some people who will not believe the promise that God has given you.

Faith is a peculiar thing. You can't touch faith! You can't see faith! Faith is something that seems impossible. Faith is something that we cannot do alone. Faith is something that we can't often explain. Faith is when the numbers don't add up. Faith is when you seek more than you are eligible for. Faith is when you try for something that you really shouldn't have. Faith is something that really cannot be explained.

Thus, the reality is that when we have faith, there will always be persons who do not believe the promise that God has placed in our lives. They say, "How is that going to work? How is this going to happen? What gave you that crazy idea? That will never happen because the numbers don't add up. You have been denied three times. Why do you keep on trying? It didn't work for me! What makes you think that it is going to work for you?"

When you step out on faith, there will be plenty of Canaanites along the way. They will show up in your home. They will show up on your job. They will show up among your friends. The Canaanites will show up!

But in the midst of the Canaanites, keep the faith. In the midst of the Canaanites, stand on God's Word. In the midst of the Canaanites, stand on the promise of God. Don't let the Canaanites deter you. Don't let the Canaanites hinder you. Don't let the Canaanites stop you.

If they say it cannot be done, keep the faith. If they say that it is impossible, keep the faith. If they say that it will never happen, keep the faith. If they say that you're crazy, keep the faith. If they say you need your head checked, keep the faith. If they say you will never reach it, keep the faith. If they say you should give up and move on to something else, keep the faith.

The God we serve makes the impossible possible. Christ makes a way out of no way! Keep the faith, because if God tells you that God is going to bless you, God will do just that. Don't let any Canaanite cause you to lose the faith and thus miss your blessing! No matter what… keep the faith!

Next, the text suggests to us that we are to worship the Lord while waiting to occupy what God has promised. When Abram reaches his destination, he has a theophany. The Lord appears to Abram in verse 7 and says, "To your offspring I will give this land." Verse 7b says, "So he built an altar there to the Lord, who has appeared to him." God informs Abram that this is the land promised to his descendants. However, God does not allow Abram to occupy the land. God just allows him to enter the land. Although Abram will not occupy the land, Abram worships the Lord.

Sometimes God informs us what the end result of our faith will be, but God does not allow us to occupy, or touch it with our own hands. Our children and their children will occupy that which we have secured for them via our faith.

From there Abram went on toward the hills of Bethel, and he pitched his tent there with Bethel on the West and Ai on the east. The writer says in verse 8b, "There he built an altar to the Lord and called on the name of the Lord."

God informs Abram that he has entered the land, but he will not occupy it. The Canaanites themselves built altar to their gods. So Abram enters the land and twice built an altar to let them know that the God he worshipped is the God who created the heavens and the earth. Abram takes possession of the land by erecting an altar.

This tells us that sometimes God informs us of our goal, but the goal has not yet become ours. The process between entering the promise and occupying the promise land are steps of faith.

The text teaches us that even though we have not occupied the promise land we must worship God, because in worshipping God, we are saying that the land will be mine. When we set out into the unfamiliar, we worship God, and when we worship God, we are saying, "God, I've seen my land of promise. I may not have possession of it now, but I believe that it will not be long before I take possession of that which you promised to me." Worshipping God says you believe that God is going to allow you to occupy that which God has promised.

Worshipping God says, "I believe the promise." Worshipping God says, "What God said will come to pass." Worshipping God acknowledges that you believe that what you now see is what God is going to have for you.

Worshipping God says, "The Canaanites may try to stop me, but I shall prevail because the Lord is on my side."

So while in the unfamiliar, worship the Lord. While stepping out on faith, worship the Lord. Proclaim that it is yours by worshipping the Lord. It might not be your possession yet, but worship the Lord. It might not have your name on it yet, but worship the Lord. You may not occupy it yet, but worship the Lord. You might not own it yet, but worship the Lord. It might not be in your custody yet, but worship the Lord. While in the midst of difficulty, worship the Lord. You might not live in it yet, but worship the Lord. It might not be yours yet, but worship the Lord. While waiting to occupy your promise land, worship the Lord.

See yourself with it and worship the Lord. See your name on it and worship the Lord. Envision that you live in it and worship the Lord. If God told you that it shall be yours, worship the Lord.

There is victory in worship. There is power in worship. There is strength in worship. There is deliverance in worship. There is healing in worship. There is success in worship.

While in the midst of unfamiliar circumstances, worship the Lord. And if you worship the Lord, the promise land shall be yours.

That's what life is. Life is not about settlement, security and placement. Life is a statement of faith that keeps us in pursuit of the promise land. Life is about the unfamiliar. Life is about God's promise. Life is about engaging the Canaanites. Life is about worshipping the Lord. Life is about reaching our promise land.

However, as soon as we reach our faith destination, another faith test comes our way. And it starts all over again. Moving into the unfamiliar. Receiving God's promise. Engaging the Canaanites. Worshipping God. Reaching our promise land. And when we reach our faith destination, it starts all over again. Moving into the unfamiliar. Receiving God's promise. Engaging the Canaanites. Worshipping God. Reaching our promise land. And when we reach our faith destination, it starts all over again.

Why? Because we are in pursuit of a promise that the Christ gave to us, which is the promise land. I'm not talking about Canaan. Canaan is not our promise land. Heaven is our promise land. God promised us heaven. This word is not our home. We are just strangers passing by.

Christ said, "In my Father's house, there are many mansions. If it were not so I would have told you. I go and prepare a place for you that where I am there ye may be also."

This world is not our home. We're just passing through. John says, "I saw a new heaven and a new earth." A New Jerusalem. That place where God dwells. That place where men will live with God. That place where God will be our God. That place where we will be God's people. That place where God will be with us. That place where God will wipe away every tear from our eyes. That place where there will be no more death. That place where there will be no more crying. That place where there will be no more pain. That place where the old will become new. The old folk said, "New hands and never feed." A place where we will never grow old. A place where every day will be Sunday, and the Sabbath will have no end.

That place where the streets are paved with gold. That place where God will be seated on the throne. Christ to His side.

That place where you will see mama and daddy. That place where you will see sister and brother.

But most of all, we will see Jesus. The One who came for us. The One who died for us. The One who was buried for us. The One who rose for us. The One who saves us. The One who delivers us. The One who heals us.

"Oh, I want to see Him, look upon His face. There to sing forever of His saving grace. On the streets of glory, let me lift my voice. Cares all past, Home at last, Ever to rejoice."

Conflict Resolution

Genesis 13:1-17 NIV

¹So Abram went up from Egypt to the Negev, with his wife and everything he had, and Lot went with him. ²Abram had become very wealthy in livestock and in silver and gold. ³From the Negev he went from place to place until he came to Bethel, to the place between Bethel and Ai where his tent had been earlier ⁴and where he had first built an altar. There Abram called on the name of the LORD. ⁵Now Lot, who was moving about with Abram, also had flocks and herds and tents. ⁶But the land could not support them while they stayed together, for their possessions were so great that they were not able to stay together. ⁷And quarreling arose between Abram's herdsmen and the herdsmen of Lot. The Canaanites and Perizzites were also living in the land at that time. ⁸So Abram said to Lot, "Let's not have any quarreling between you and me, or between your herdsmen and mine, for we are brothers. ⁹Is not the whole land before you? Let's part company. If you go to the left, I'll go to the right; if you go to the right, I'll go to the left." ¹⁰Lot looked up and saw that the whole plain of the Jordan was well watered, like the garden of the LORD, like the land of Egypt, toward Zoar. (This was before the LORD destroyed Sodom and Gomorrah.) ¹¹So Lot chose for himself the whole plain of the Jordan and set out toward the east. The two men parted company: ¹²Abram lived in the land of Canaan, while Lot lived among the cities of the plain and pitched his tents near Sodom. ¹³Now the men of Sodom were wicked and were sinning greatly against the LORD. ¹⁴The LORD said to Abram after Lot had parted from him, "Lift up your eyes from where you are and look north and south, east and west. ¹⁵All the land that you see I will give to you and your offspring forever. ¹⁶I will make your offspring like the dust of the earth, so that if anyone could count the dust, then your offspring could be counted. ¹⁷Go, walk through the length and breadth of the land, for I am giving it to you."

Just the other day I was in conversation with an individual in higher education. She stated to me that a vice-president at her college brought a job announcement to her office demanding that she apply for it. He said, "Rochelle, you need to apply for this. You meet the qualifications, and you will do an excellent job."

She hesitated to do so because she was concerned about her loyalty to her college. She said to him, "What will it look like if I leave here after having been in the position for only two years? The college paid for my certification, and even though I qualify for the job, I do not think that it would be right for me to go to the other side of town to work for another college." He said to her, "I never stay in a job more than two or three years before I apply for another position. I know where I want to be at a certain age, and I know how I am going to get there. I only work in positions for two or three years. Go ahead and apply. You will do a great job." With that he turned and walked out of her office.

She asked me, "What should she do?" I told her to pray about it. Then I began to think about loyalty in our society. There seems to be little or no loyalty in our society today. We live in such a fast-paced world. We are in a rush to get to work. We are in a rush to get home. We are in a rush to get to the gym. We are in a rush to get to the grocery store. We are pushed on our jobs to produce and produce more, and when we don't, our jobs are in jeopardy. And because we live in such a fast-paced world, this idea of loyalty has been thrown out of the window.

Where are the days when people went to work for a company straight out of high school or college and worked within the company until retirement? Where have the days gone when people chose to work up the company ladder instead of going to a rival for a better promotion and a higher salary? Where are the days when people waited their turn for promotion, waiting patiently for their superiors to retire? Where have the days gone when company loyalty mattered?

We live in a world today where people jump from one thing to another, from one company to another. People are so eager to be promoted that they are not willing to wait in line. People will take company secrets to another company and use that as a means to negotiate compensation. There seems to be no loyalty in our world today.

Our fast-paced world and lack of loyalty have even entered into our relationships. People today move from one relationship to another just like they open a bag of potato chips. When something goes wrong, people bail out. There is no working it out. There is no notion of compromising. There is no such thing as sitting down and coming to an amicable solution. People just disagree and move on without even trying to work things out.

We all know that conflict is a way of life. We cannot avoid conflict. We can't shun disagreements. We can't stay away from disputes. More often than not, there will be times of discord, dispute and tension.

When these situations arise, we can't just leave, quit and go our separate ways without coming to some type of resolution. We have to learn to handle conflict. We have to learn to appropriately manage disputes. We have to become skilled at coming to solutions when dealing with controversy.

Let me just say that sometimes relationships work out and sometimes they don't. This is the focus of this sermon. The focus of this sermon is how to handle separation when conflict breaks out. Sometimes, whether fortunately or unfortunately, relationships just don't work out. Whether or not relationships work out is not the issue. How they are worked out is what is important?

I want to suggest to you that our text for today helps us with conflict resolution. It helps us to understand what we must do when relationships don't work out.

There has been a severe famine in the land of Canaan. During the famine, Abram is in Egypt. His wife, Sarai, is a very beautiful woman. Abram fears for his life so he tells Sarai to tell the Egyptians that she is his sister and not his wife. Abram says, "I know what a beautiful woman you are. When the Egyptians see you, they will say, 'This is his wife. Then they will kill me but will let you live. Say you are my sister so that I will be treated well for your sake and my life will be spared because of you." (Chapter 12:13)

When the Egyptians saw how beautiful Sarai was, they tell Pharaoh. Sarai is taken to Pharaoh's palace. Abram is treated well because of Sarai, so well that he acquired sheep and cattle, male and female donkeys, menservants and maidservants, and camels.

Yet, the Lord is not pleased with what has happened. The Lord inflicted serious diseases on Pharaoh and his household because of Abram's wife, Sarai. Pharaoh summons Abram and says, "What have you done to me? Why didn't you tell me she was your wife? Why did you say, 'She is my sister,' so that I took her to be my wife? Now then, here is your wife. Take her and go!" (Chapter 12:18-19) "Then Pharaoh gave orders about Abram to his men, and they sent him on his way, with his wife and everything he had." (Chapter 12:20)

The famine is now over. Abram is back in Canaan, the land of promise. Abram takes everything he has with him, and Lott is with him as well.

Not only did Abram have sheep and cattle, male and female donkeys, menservants and maidservants and camels, he also has become wealthy in silver and gold. This is the first time that the Bible mentions silver and gold. Abram is blessed with much silver and gold, which implies that he had business partners among the Egyptians with operations in mining and the process of refining precious metals. Abram was a wealthy man.

Abram enters the promise land. First, he goes to Negev (neg'ev), then from place to place, until he came to Bethel or a place between Bethel (uhl) and Ai. This is the same place where he had settled in Chapter 12. The same place where he built his first altar to the Lord in Canaan.

Abram's nephew, Lott, is moving to and fro with Abram. Lot also had flocks, herds and tents. Everything seems to be going well. However, there was a problem. The problem was that "the land could not support them while they stayed together, for their possessions were so great that they were not able to stay together. And quarreling arose between Abram's herdsmen and the herdsmen of Lot." (verses 5-6)

The land had not recovered from the drought. There were not enough pastures and watering places among them because of the drought. Both Abram and Lot were nomadic, so they needed to feed themselves, their servants, their flocks and their herds, and without pastures and watering places, this was hard to do. Their pastureland and watering places were scarce, but their substance is great. They could not dwell together and support their households at the same time.

It became so difficult to dwell together that the herdsmen of Abram and Lott began to quarrel. To add to this, "the Canaanites and the Perizzites were also living in the land." (verse 7) The situation is complicated because there are even fewer wells and fertile land because the Canaanites and the Perizzites (per'uh-zit) occupied the land as well. The Canaanites lived in the lowlands and had built walled towns. The Perizzites lived in the highlands in the hills and woods of Palestine. They lived in the open country and had built villages, and there was simply no land to share.

Lott participates in Abram's wealth and obedience. If not for Abram,

Lott would not have had the wealth that he had. But with this wealth comes conflict. Wealth can be a blessing. Yet, the problem is that so often we desire good things in the wrong way. And this causes people to fall out.

So Abram says to Lot, "Let's not have any quarreling between you and me, or between your herdsmen and mine, for we are brothers. Is not the whole land before you? Let's part company. If you go to the left, I'll go to the right; if you go to the right, I'll go to the left." (verse 8-9)

Being amicable and harmonious is the first thing we should do when handling conflict and/or going our separate ways. This means the probability of renouncing our rights and letting the one we are quarreling with get the first piece of the pie.

Quarreling among nomads over pasture and wells was not uncommon. History teaches us that it was common for families to separate. The text does not blame Abram or Lott for the separation. It is how they separated that we want to concentrate on.

Abram takes the initiative to settle the interfamily squabble. He does so for two reasons. First, they are family—uncle and nephew. Therefore, there should be no squabbling among them. This even includes the herdsmen, because they are an extension of the family unit. Second, Abram is interested in peace. He says, "Let's not have any quarreling between you and me." So Abram says, "If you go to the left, I'll go to the right and if you go to the right, I will go to the left."

Abram does not want quarreling among the family. In addition, Abram perceived Lott's face was not towards him as usual. In other words, Abram knew that Lott had his eyes set on pastures and water, and Abram wanted to divert collision, so Abram says, "Let's separate."

The story hasn't changed much today. Families are still fighting over land and possessions. Let the mother or father of the family die and see how children fight over what mama and daddy left behind. Children often are found trying to grab what they can while mama or daddy is still alive. That's why I encourage you to do your Will Planning, stating explicitly who gets what, when and where. Families are still quarreling over possessions today.

Not only families, but we also find society quarreling over possessions today. All we have to do is turn on CNN and we will hear of people fighting over land and/or possessions. Surely, we will find ourselves in the midst of situations such as these.

When we do, the question becomes, are you like Abram or like Lott? Are you seeking to squash conflict or do you have your eyes set on the prize? Does family mean more to you than the possession you see? Are you like Abram, who says, "Man, you choose what you want, and what you don't want, I will take? Or are you like Lott? Have you already set your eyes on the piece of the pie?

Are you like Abram or Lott? There are those who defuse and those who incite. Which one are you? Are you one who defuses conflicts? Or are you the one who incites them? Are you the one who seeks to resolve conflict? Or are you the one who aggravates the situation? Are you the one who will try to come to a peaceful resolution? Or are you the one who will provoke the situation even further? Are you the one who puts out fires? Or are you the one who incites, stirs up things and provokes the action?

All of us as Christians should be the ones who try to bring peaceful solutions to volatile situations.

The fact of the matter is that we will often find ourselves in the midst of arguments and disagreements. That's just a part of life.

To be truthful, there are times when the best thing to do is go our separate ways. Sometimes things don't work out. Sometimes relationships do end. Sometimes friendships have run their course. Sometimes we do have to move on to another place of employment. Sometimes we have stayed too long. When these situations occur, we have to separate. We have to part. We have to disconnect. We have to split. We have to break up. We have to divide possessions. We do have to break away.

Sometimes, breaking away is good for our mental, spiritual, and physical well-being. The issue is not that we have broken away. The issue is how we handle the break-up. The way we handle the break-up has salvific implications. The way we handle the split can strengthen or crush our Christian witness. So we have to be careful how we separate. We have to be mindful of the way we split. We have to think how we are going to handle things after the departure before we depart, because the world is watching to see how we handle situations such as these.

So the first thing we must do is do what Abram did. We must renounce our right for the sake of an amicable settlement.

We have to be the bigger person. We have to be the most spiritual Christian. We have to be the example of Christ. We may have to give some things up. We may have to let others make the first move. We may have to let others choose first while we receive what's left.

We must keep in mind that our blessings may not come in that which we can see; our blessings may come from how we handle the situation. There are no blessings in greed. There are no blessings in fighting over material things. There is no promise land in ruining relationships over things that will rot and decay. We can't take money and possessions with us. Therefore, the thing that should be most important to us is how we handle conflicts! How we handle the break-up! How we handle the splitting up of property!

When handling conflict and separation, the first thing we should do is renounce our rights for the sake of an amicable, friendly, good-natured, harmonious and cordial agreement. The least we can do is be cordial to one another.

Secondly, Lot chooses his territory out of eagerness, lust, and greed.

Abram said, "Is not the whole land before you? Let's part company. If you go to the left, I'll go to the right; if you go to the right, I'll go to the left." Abram, older and greater, cedes choice of the portions to Lot.

"Lot looked up and saw that the whole plain of the Jordan was well watered, like the garden of the Lord, like the land of Egypt, towards Zoar." (verse 10)

It is said that when the land was divided that the first one to choose chose land as far as he could see. Lot looks up and chooses the entire Jordon valley. The Jordan valley is full of wells of water like the Garden of Eden that Abram and Lot had heard so much about. There are water wells everywhere. The plain of the Jordon was well irrigated, like Egypt. Egypt was well irrigated by the Nile and the canals of the Nile. The land that Lott chose had water wells like the four rivers in the Garden of Eden.

The plain of the Jordan was in the low country with two river sources. The largest was the river in Palestine with 200 miles, more than twenty-seven rapids and water pouring into the lake Merom and then into the Sea of Galilee.

Lott saw all of this and he thought for a happy future. He lifts up his eyes and he looks forward and sees the plain of the Jordon, and the Bible says, "So Lot chose for himself the whole plain of the Jordon and set out toward the east. The two men parted company." (verse 11)

Yet, the writer gives us clues that the land that Lot thought was fertile was not fertile at all. The writer says in verse 13, "Now the men of Sodom were wicked and were sinning greatly against the Lord." Lott lived among the cities of the plain and pitched his tents near Sodom.

In the very next chapter, we find Abram having to rescue Lot from the wickedness that took place in Sodom. Our text for today doesn't suggest this, but we can imply this from Chapter 14. When people part, it doesn't have to get nasty. You can still go your separate ways, and when the person you have separated from needs help or is in a major dilemma, you can come and rescue them from whatever they are going through. Separation doesn't mean that one becomes enemies. It simply means that one cannot co-habit together in the manner that one once did. So you can part company and love the person or institution, so that when they or it needs help you can come to the rescue.

Lot is on the Bethel plateau, and thus he has an extensive view of Palestine. Lot has a chance the view the whole country. Lot's does, but his eyes deceived him. He thought that he had chosen Eden, but he chose Sodom, and Sodom is not Eden. His eyes were filled with earthly desires. He chose what his eyes saw and not what God had chosen for him. Therefore, he finds himself getting in trouble and barely making it out of Sodom.

Our eyes can be full of deception. Our grandparents knew this. This is why they said, "Everything that looks good ain't good for you." They said, "The grass ain't always greener on the other side." They knew that everything that looked good wasn't good. They knew that some things that smelled nice, after a while, would not be as nice as they first smelled. They knew that everything that looked beautiful wasn't beautiful. They knew that every 36-24-36 figure would not stay that way, so instead of looking at the body, they told us to look at the heart and what was in the head.

So many of us are allured by beauty and fertility. And because we see beauty and fertility, we pay no attention to other considerations. The eyes can deceive. Our eyes can tell us that the land is good, but the land can be just as wicked as it can be.

We can't trust our eyes. Our eyes are trained to the Western world, where we are told that the bigger the better, the more fertile the more lucrative, the larger the more respect we receive. Yet, our eyes can be deceptive.

Jesus said this. He said, "If your eye causes you to sin, take that eye out because it is better to live with one eye than to burn in hell."

Our eyes can deceive us; therefore, we don't need to choose our own land. We need to let God choose the land for us. Every time we choose, we make a mistake. Every time we choose, we make the wrong decision. Every time we choose, we do more harm than we do good. Every time we choose, wickedness comes forth. Every time we choose, we end up running in the opposite direction. Every time we choose, we mess up.

So instead of choosing your own land, let God choose it for you. Instead of you choosing your husband, let God choose him for you. Instead of you choosing your wife, let God choose her for you. Instead of you choosing the school you will go to, let God choose it for you. Instead of you deciding when and what you will buy, let God choose for you. Instead of you deciding what job you will apply for, let God choose for you.

When God chooses for you, you will never go wrong. It will never be a mistake. You will never regret your choice. You will never have to run in the opposite direction.

When God chooses, the land will be plentiful. The land will be fertile. The grass will grow. Water will be everywhere. Happiness will prevail. Joy will run through your soul. Blessings will be in abundance. Your life live will prosper.

Don't you choose your land! Let God choose the land for you.

Thirdly, Abram, unlike Lot, walked by faith and not by sight. Abram said, "Lot choose the land you want."

Abram lived in the land of Canaan while Lot lived among the cities of the plain and pitched his tents near the wicked city of Sodom.

After Lot had parted from Abram, the Lord said to Abram, "Lift up your eyes from where you are and look north and south, east and west. All the land you see I will give to you and your offspring like the dust of the earth, so that if anyone could count the dust, then your offspring could be counted. Go, walk through the length and breadth of the land, for I am giving it to you."

The Lord says, "Abram, lift up your eyes." Abram is between Bethel and Ai on one of the mountain peaks. He has a commanding view of almost the entire country. He looked Northward and saw the hills that divide Judea from the rich plains of Samaria. He looked southward as far as to the Hebron range. He looked eastward in the direction of the dark mountain wall of Moab, down through the rich ravine that leads from the central hills of Palestine to the valley of the Jordan and across the very circle where Lot now resides. The land that God will give him includes the land that Lot has chosen. He looks westward toward the sea. He is standing on the stony but fertile plateau between Bethel and Ai.

And the Lord says, "All of this that you see I will give to you and to your offspring. Your offspring will be like the dust of the earth. If anyone can count the dust, then the will be able to count your offspring.

God says, "Abram, go, walk through the length and breadth of the land, for I am giving it to you." God will bless Abram and his descendants with innumerable land.

Abram lived in the land many years, grew old and died, but his offspring got the blessings of it as well. This land was promised to Abram, and he believed in the promise. Abram, unlike Lot, did not walk by sight; Abram walked by faith.

Are you like Abram? Or are you like Lot? Do you walk by sight? Or do you walk by faith? We must be like Abram. We must walk by faith and not by sight. Our grandparents walked by faith and not by sight. They didn't have many material possessions, but they had faith. My paternal grandfather died when my daddy was twelve. He left my grandmother Emma with twelve children. Yet, she will tell you that she was not alone. She had God, and she had faith. Daddy told me the other day that there was no doubt about it, that they were the poorest family around. They had an old ragged house to live in, but my grandmother had faith. They didn't have much to eat, but they always had something to eat because my grandmother had faith. They always had clothes on their back because she had faith. They always had shoes on their feet because she had faith. All twelve finished high school, and some went to college because she had faith. We must walk by faith and not by sight.

Faith is a peculiar thing. We defined faith last week as "moving from the familiar to the unfamiliar." You can't touch faith! You can't see faith! You can't smell faith! You can't taste faith! You can't hear faith. Faith is something that you believe on the inside. Faith is having confidence in something that you believe only God can do. If you can do it, it doesn't require faith. Faith is something that seems impossible. Faith is something that we cannot do alone. Faith is something that we often can't explain. Faith is when the numbers don't add up. Faith is when you seek more than you are eligible for. Faith is when you try for something that you really shouldn't have. Faith is something that really cannot be explained. "We walk by faith and not by sight."

God is saying to us today, "Rise and Walk! Survey your inheritance with the calm assurance that it is yours." Some of us are still trying to hold on to that which we should have let go a long time ago because we are scared of that unfamiliar territory. But I stopped by here to tell you to step out on faith. The Lord will provide! Some of you are still in situations God told you to get out of year ago. You are still in those situations because you are scared of that which you cannot see. I stopped by here to tell you the Lord will provide! Step out on faith! God told you to resign from that position last year, but you are still there. You better step out on faith! For the Lord will provide. Some of you are still in relationships that God did not put together and those relationships are pulling you down, exhausting your energy and zapping your joy. God has told you time and time to get out and regain your sanity, but you are still there because you are thinking, "I will hold on to what I have because the next one might be a lot worse." Baby, you better step out on faith and leave now. The Lord will provide. God says, "I have given it to you.

Our seniors put it this way, "The Lord will make a way out of no way. The Lord will perform miracles with wonders to perform. If you take one step, God will take two."

When you depart from that which God tells you to leave behind, God will bless you with more when you depart than you would have had if you stayed. Sometimes you have to part company with people in order to receive the abundance of blessings that God wants to give in your life.

When you walk by faith, you will be blessed in ways you never thought or imagined. When you let God choose your land, God will give you more land than you ever thought you would receive. When you walk by faith, you're eyes will see blessings coming far from the north and the south, the east and the west. When you walk by faith, God will say, "All this land is yours." When you walk by faith, God will give you what God promised you. When you walk by faith, you offspring will be like the dust of the earth. When you walk by faith, possessions will multiply. When you walk by faith, you will have more than enough. When you walk by faith, man will not be able to count your blessings. When you walk by faith, you will not be able to measure the length nor the breadth of the land that God is going to give you.

Our grandparents didn't have much, but they had faith. I would rather have faith than all the possessions in the world. We need to walk by faith and not by sight.

By faith, miracles happen! By faith, deliverance takes place! By faith, chains are broken! By faith, persons are liberated! By faith, homes are purchased! By faith, promotions are received! By faith, children are raised! By faith, money is saved! By faith, degrees are granted! By faith, addicts are cured! By faith, mortgages are paid! By faith, lights stay on! By faith, food is placed on the table. By faith, clothes are placed on backs! By faith, our grandparents made it! By faith, mama and daddy survived! By faith, we shall prevail!

By faith, Jesus came down forty and two generations. By faith, He proclaimed to be the savior of the world. By faith, He was arrested. By faith, He was mocked and spat on! By faith, He went to that old rugged cross. By faith, He was crucified for my sins and your sins! By faith, He was put in the tomb for three days. By faith, He rose on the third day with all power in His hands.

Walk by faith and not by sight!

A Crisis of Faith

Genesis 15:1-6 NIV

[1]*After this, the word of the LORD came to Abram in a vision: "Do not be afraid, Abram. I am your shield, your very great reward."* [2]*But Abram said, "O Sovereign LORD, what can you give me since I remain childless and the one who will inherit my estate is Eliezer of Damascus?"* [3]*And Abram said, "You have given me no children; so a servant in my household will be my heir."* [4]*Then the word of the LORD came to him: "This man will not be your heir, but a son coming from your own body will be your heir."* [5]*He took him outside and said, "Look up at the heavens and count the stars—if indeed you can count them." Then he said to him, "So shall your offspring be."* [6]*Abram believed the LORD, and he credited it to him as righteousness.*

A few weeks ago, we defined faith as "moving from the familiar to the unfamiliar." Last week we defined faith as "letting God choose your land for you."

I want to suggest to you that all humankind places his or her faith in something. The issue is not whether we have faith or not. The issue is where we place our faith. In whom do we place our ultimate trust?

For example, every time we step on the brakes of our vehicles, we display tremendous faith in gadgets that most of us know nothing about. Every time we need lights in our homes, we demonstrate faith when we go to the light switch on the wall. When we go to the sink to wash our hands, we reveal faith when we turn on the faucet, believing that water will begin to flow. When our refrigerators don't cool, we call the repairman, proving that we trust him to work on our refrigerators. When we go to a restaurant, we trust the chefs who prepare our food for nourishment of our bodies, even though we never see them, nor do we know them. We have the faith that our food will be properly cooked and the taste will be to our liking. Every time we go to our financial institutions, we trust that the money that we deposit into our accounts will be there when we go back to get it. We even trust our financial institutions to safeguard our hard-earned monies with the expectation that we will receive a little interest in return.

It is not that we do not have faith. All of us have faith. The real question is: In whom do we place our faith? Either we trust God or we trust something or someone else.

This week I want to define faith as "the ability to see into the future." So many people can only see in the present. Many people cannot see, or refuse to see, into the future. Many people see only what is in the present. Faith is not that which we can see. Faith is that which we cannot see. Faith is not what we can touch today. Faith is something that we will be able to touch in the future. Faith is not that which we taste today. Faith is something that we will be able to taste in the days to come.

So many people miss their blessings simply because they cannot see into the future. They can see only what is present today. And when people can see only today, their lack of faith restricts what God wants to do in the time to come.

Every now and then we face a crisis of belief. We have faith but our faith sometimes turns into doubt. A crisis of belief means that we have faith one moment and then the next moment we doubt the faith that we just expressed. God gives us a promise. We say, "Yes, Lord, I believe that you will give me what you have promised." Then the very next minute we say, "Lord, how is that going to happen?" So many times we are tossed to and fro, from that which God has said will happen to what the world defines as reality.

We do have crises of belief. We believe the promise then doubt the promise because we wonder how the promise will come to fruition. We doubt the promise because we cannot see into the future. When these times exist, we must not doubt the promise because God has promised to do it, and when God promises to do it, God will do it.

The chapter in which our text for today resides has been said to be the most pivotal in the Abraham tradition. Scholars have said that this is the most important chapter in the tradition. Scholars have also said that this is the oldest statement of the Abrahamic faith and others that derive from it.

In our text for preachment today, we find Abram coming off a great military victory. Lot is living in Sodom. Sodom and Gomorrah are defeated by enemy kings. Lott and his possessions are carried away. One who had escaped came and told Abram what had happened. When Abram heard that his relative was taken into captivity, he calls the 318 trained men in his household and he went in pursuit. (See how the Lord has kept his promise to Abram!) During the night, Abram divided his men to attack these four kings who had Lot captive, and he routed them, pursuing them for quite a distance.

Abram recovered all the goods and brought Lott, his possessions, the women and the other people back. When Abram returned from his victory, the king of Sodom came out to meet him. Then Melchizedek, the king of Salem, who was allied with the king of Sodom, brought bread and wine, and he as the priest of the Most High God blessed Abram saying, "Blessed be Abram by God Most High, Creator of heaven and earth. And blessed be God Most High, who delivered your enemies into your hand."

The Bible says, "Then Abram gave him a tenth of everything."

The King of Sodom said to Abram, "Give me the people and keep the goods for yourself." Abram said to the king of Sodom, "I have raised my hand to the Lord, God Most High, Creator of heaven and earth, and have taken an oath that I will accept nothing belonging to you, not even a thread or the thong of a sandal, so that you will never be able to say, 'I made Abram rich.' I will accept nothing but what my men have eaten and the share that belong to the men who went with me. Let them have their share."

"After this the word of the Lord came to Abram in a vision." The Lord said, "Don't be afraid, Abram. I am your shield, your very great reward." Abram has a crisis of belief. Abram says, "O Sovereign Lord, what can you give me since I remain childless and the one who will inherit my estate is Eliezer of Damascus? You have given me no children; so a servant in my household will be my heir."

The Word of the Lord comes to Abram. "This man will not be your heir, but a son coming from your own body will be your heir." The Lord takes Abram outside and said, "Look up at the heavens and count the stars—if you indeed can count them." Then the Lord said, "So shall your offspring be." The writer says, "Abram believed the Lord and the Lord credited it to him as righteous."

First, a crisis of faith means that we don't believe the future that God has promised to us. Abram is fearful of the future, and thus he seems to forget God's promise, which is that his reward will be great.

The Word of the Lord came to Abram in a vision. The Word says, "Do not be afraid, Abram. I am your shield, your very great reward."

Abram and Sarai are barren. They have no children. God comes to Abram and tells him to "leave his country, his people, and his father's household and go to the land that God will show him." The Lord tells him, "I will make you into a great nation and I will bless you; I will make your name great, and you will be a blessing. I will bless those who bless you and whoever curses you I will curse; and all peoples on earth will be blessed through you."

Abram leaves and does what the Lord tells him to do. He arrives in the land of Canaan. He has just been granted a great military victory. He has stood on the promise that God has given him. "I will make you into a great nation and I will bless you." "I will make your offspring like the dust of the earth, so that if anyone could count the dust, then your offspring could be counted."

Yet, there is anxiety on Abram's part because there is no offspring. He has no children. Sarai is barren. Abram is concerned because it seems to him that he will die childless and have no name on earth. Abram must have been thinking, "How in the world is the Lord going to make me into a great nation when I have no heir? How in the world is the Lord going to make my offspring like the dust of the earth when I have no son who can create further offspring? What type of inheritance will I have if I have no inheritor, no children? How can a childless man pass on an inheritance?"

Abram is fearful of the future. He must have concluded that there will be no change.

If barrenness prevails, there will be no promise. God seems to know that Abram is concerned about the promise being fulfilled, so God speaks with a word that reestablishes the promise. God says, "Do not be afraid, Abram. I am your shield, your very great reward."

The reward is specified in verse 18. The writer says, "On that day the Lord made a covenant with Abram and said, 'To your descendants I give this land...'" Abram is in the land, and God has to remind him of the promise that has been made. The promise is the land. God says, "Great is your reward."

"Reward" in the Hebrew many times suggests "economic settlement" and even "wage." But this time, "reward" implies a gift and not something done in exchange. The reward is not earned. It is not a prize earned. The reward is a special recognition given to the king's faithful servant who has performed a risky or bold service.

Abram showed faith when he left his own country and God says, "Great is your reward because you have been faithful."

The reward calls for us to walk by faith, even while living in the midst of barrenness.

The first crisis of faith that we face is when we have to deal with the fact that the promise has not become reality. We all deal with this. We have the promise but there seems to be no sight in the future that the promise will come to pass.

This is a crisis of faith. The promise is that the land shall be yours, but the land is not in your possession. The promise is that you will receive a job, but there are no jobs available. The promise is that you will receive the promotion, but all positions that will grant a promotion are occupied. The promise is that you will be healed of your sickness, but the doctors say that there is nothing else they can do. The promise is that doors of opportunity will be opened, but every door you try to go through seems to be closed. The promise is that blessings will come from heaven, but as of to this day the doors of heaven seem to be closed. The promise is that your prayer will be answered, but as of right this moment you have heard nothing from the Lord who promised to give you an answer. God has promised us fertility, but we are still living in barrenness, and it does not seem that barrenness will end any time soon.

When it comes to faith, all of us face the fear of whether or not the promise will come true. This is a crisis of faith.

Yet, when we reach this crisis of faith, a Word from the Lord comes which says, "Do not be afraid. I am your shield. Great is your reward."

Don't be afraid! For God is your shield. God is your protection. God is your defense. God is there to safeguard you. God is there to be your shelter.

If you keep the faith, great is your reward. Remove the fear from your life. Let go of your anxiety. God has your back. What God says will come to pass. It may not come to pass when you want it to, but it will come to pass. Great is your reward if you keep the faith. If you keep the faith, the door will be opened. If you keep the faith, the blessing will come. If you keep the faith, your prayer will be answered. If you keep the faith, fertility will come. If you keep the faith, the promise will come to pass. If you keep the faith, the land will be yours. If you keep the faith, the money will appear. If you have the faith, a job will be yours. If you keep the faith, the promotion will be given. If you keep the faith, healing will take place.

Don't be fearful of the future. Hold on to the promise. It will come. What God promised, God has already granted.

Secondly, a crisis of faith always includes protest. We see Abram's protest. Abram says, "O Sovereign Lord, what can you give me since I remain childless and the one who will inherit my estate is Eliezer of Damascus?" Then Abram says, "You have given me no children; so a servant in my household will be my heir."

Abram has heard the Divine promise, but there is no fruit. He is childless. He has heard the promise of land but sees no future because there is no heir. He sees himself only as a barren vessel. Abram believes that without an heir, his faith is as good as dead.

Abram is unable to see forward, so he proposes to God his own solution: *You have given me no children; so a servant in my household will be my heir. Eliezer of Damascus is my closest slave and he will inherit everything I have because, Lord, even though you say that I will not remain barren I am still that way because I have no children. Lord, you are Sovereign, but how can a childless man pass on an inheritance? The only way he can do it is pass it on to his slave.*

In biblical times, the absence of a child or relative meant that the slave was granted rights to the inheritance, because he was considered part of the family.

Abram doubts the promise God has made him. He says, "What good is the land, if I have no children to pass them on to?" Abram does not concentrate on what God can give. He concentrates on what God has not given. God has not given him an heir. Abram does not doubt that there will be an heir because the heir is Eliezer. He doubts that an heir will be his child.

So Abram's default is Eliezer. Abram begins to doubt God's promise, and in doing so he reverts to worldly principles of inheritance. His heir will be his slave. Abram takes the future into his own hands. He relies on human laws, human principals, human activity and human strategy.

There are times in our lives when we are just like Abram. We have a crisis of belief. We doubt the promise of God. God has given us the promise, but we have not seen the fruit of the promise. We are still barren. We are still without. We say we have faith, but after a while we begin to doubt God because we believe that God has not done what God said he would do.

Unable to see the future we move forward with our own plan. We come up with our own solution: "Lord, you said you would, but as of yet you haven't, so I'm going to take matters into my own hands." We don't concentrate on what God has given. God has given us the promise. We concentrate on what God has not given. So we take matters into our own hands. We revert to human principals. We rely on human laws. We go to human solutions and principals. We become active because we think that God is not working. We go to human strategy when God has already told us what the strategy is.

In every situation that requires faith, there is this crisis of doubt. We doubt God.

Yet, when we step out on faith, this doubt must quickly move back to faith. The reality is that if we could have done it ourselves we wouldn't have needed God. The fact that we need God means that we could not do it ourselves. And when we try to do it ourselves we mess up, just like Abram. Abram took matters into his own hands when he slept with Hagar and she gave birth to Ishmael when he doubted that God would give Sarai, his wife, a child. Ishmael, the Palestinians, and Abram and Isaac, the Israelites, are still fighting, and their fighting affects the entire world today. Abram is dead and we are still dealing with Abram's doubt today.

Doubt has lasting consequences. Why do we doubt the only One who can give us the promise? Why do we doubt the God who is the only One who can make it happen? Why do we doubt the God who took nothing and made everything we see?

When we doubt God, we doubt the One who is Sovereign. We doubt the One who is supreme. We doubt the One who created the world and everything in it. We doubt the One who is Alpha and Omega, the Beginning and the End. We doubt the God who holds the world in God's hands. We doubt the One who knows all things, who is present everywhere, who can be here and there at the same time. We doubt the One who has all power in God's hands. We doubt the One who is the same yesterday, today and forevermore. We doubt the One who has been there in the past and will be there in the future. We doubt the One who has provided for us before and will provide for us again. We doubt the One who has picked us up before. We doubt the One who has done the impossible in our lives.

The One who granted the promise in the past is the One who will grant the promise now. Don't take matters into your own hands. You will mess up every time. The Lord will provide. "He may not come when you want Him to, but He will be there right on time."

Thirdly, when we doubt, God always counters our doubt with a Word. Abram says, "Lord, what can you give me since I remain childless and the one who will inherit my estate is Eliezer of Damascus? You have given me no children; so a servant in my household will be my heir." Abram doubts.

Yet, God does not remain silent. The writer says, "Then the word of the Lord came (again) to him: 'This man will not be your heir, but a son coming from your own body will be your heir.' The Lord takes Abram outside and said, 'Look up at the heavens and count the stars—if indeed you can count them.'" Then the Lord said to Abram, "So shall your offspring be."

A word again comes to Abram as he faces this crisis of belief. God says, "This man will not be your heir, but a son coming from your own body will be heir... Look up at the heavens and count the stars—if indeed you can count them... So shall your offspring be."

Abram is unable to see forward. He promises his own solution. But God rejects his solution. God says, "Eliezer will not be your heir." God promises God's own solution. "You will have a son and your offspring will be as numerous as the starts in the sky." God announces to Abram that, even though you don't have an heir yet, I will give you not only a heir, but I will give you so many descendants that you cannot even begin to count them.

God counters Abram's doubt with a Word. This is not a sign, but this is a revelation. God reveals to Abram that he will have a son, and God reveals to him that his offspring will be as numerous as the stars in the sky.

God makes it clear to Abram that God is God. At a dark time in Abram's life, God gives a Word that reminds him of the promise that God has given.

It is when we face a crisis of faith that God steps in and counters our doubt with a Word. It is when the days are the darkest and our faith is in crisis mode that God steps in and give us a solution. It is when we go from faith to doubt, from belief to unbelief and back to faith again that God steps in and says, "This is what I'm going to do."

It is when we face this crisis of faith that God takes the initiative and promises a solution. It is when we are not able to see the forest for the trees that God says, "So shall it be." It is when we take the initiative and attempt to move forward in the way that we think we should go that God says, "Hold up! Wait a minute! Let me show you what I am going to do."

It is when we face this crisis of faith that God gives a revelation. God reveals what God is going to do. God discloses to us how it will happen. God takes us and show us what will happen and it surprises us because it was nobody but God.

God says, "You will have." God says, "It will happen." God says, "Be patient, I'm going to move." God says, "Not your time, but my time. Not your way, but my way." God says, "Just be still. I'm working things out." God says, "Be still! I'm working it out as we speak." God says, "Trouble won't last always. I'm going to open the door. The future I promised will come to pass." God says, "Let me show you what I am going to do." God says, "So shall your offspring be. So shall your life be. So shall that child be. So shall the end result be. So shall your business be. So shall that promotion be. So shall the consequence be. So shall that relationship be. Look up! So shall the solution be."

At the darkest moment of our crisis of belief, God steps in with a Word. And I thank God for the Word. I praise God for the Word. Because when I began to doubt the promise that God has given, the word gives me the calm assurance that God has not forgotten about me. "So shall your offspring be." God always speaks to our concerns when there is a crisis of belief.

Finally, we must believe the Word God has given. Abram accepted the promise. The writer says, "Abram believed the Lord, and he credited it to him as righteousness."

God's image moves from dust to stars. God said in Chapter 13 that Abram descendants will be as numerous as the dust of the earth. Here God says that Abram's descendants will be as numerous as the stars in the heavens. The stars suggest stability and security that dust does not.

God is the only One who could give a revelation like this. It is clear to Abram that the revelation is from God. Who would tell him that he would have a son when Sarai was barren? Nobody but God! Who would take him outside and tell him to look up into the heavens, count the starts if he can, and then say, "So shall your offspring be?" Nobody but God!

Abram was able to differentiate between the concrete visible and the promised. Abram believed God. God is the One to which his faith clings. Abram believes. He says, "God's got it, so I am just going to chill and relax and wait on God."

Abram believed and God credited him as righteous. God reckoned him as righteous. In biblical days, crediting declared that a gift had been properly offered. God functions as priest and declares that Abram is righteous. Abram is righteous means that by his faith he is made right with God. By virtue of Abram's faith, he becomes righteous.

We must be like Abram. We will have crises of faith. Human nature just assures us that there will be times when we will doubt God. I know that it should not happen, but it does. Yet, when God speaks a Word to us, that Word is so powerful that we have no other choice but to declare, "I believe." We have to be able to differentiate between that which we see and that which God has promised.

You can't see, touch, hear, smell or taste faith! Faith is something that resides on the inside. Faith is something that we believe. Faith is the calm assurance that everything is going to be all right. Faith is the belief that God will fix it; that God will solve it, that God will do it.

And it is our faith that puts us in the right relationship with God. Belief does that. Belief puts us in the right relationship with God. It is our faith that makes us righteous before God.

Our faith must say, "Lord, I believe. Lord, I believe! Lord, I believe! I don't fear anymore! I'm not afraid anymore! I don't doubt anymore! I distrust Your Word no longer! Lord, I believe! I believe Your promise! I believe Your plan! I believe Your strategy! I believe Your principles! I want it Your way! I believe Your future for my life! No more barrenness! No more infertility! No more non-productivity. I believe! I believe your promise! I can see into the future because I believe! I believe the land will be mine! I believe I will be fruitful! My children will be blessed! The promise will come to fruition! No more doubt! I will be granted what You said, and my blessing will be as numerous as the stars in the sky! I believe that I will be stable! I believe that I will be secure. I believe that I will be safe. I believe that God will shelter me. I believe that I will obtain it. I am confident that God will provide it! I believe that God can! I believe God will!

I believe that God is able.

Able to deliver me! Able to provide what I need! Able to do that which I can't explain! Able to move in ways with wonders to perform! Able to heal! Able to deliver! Able to heal! Able to move! Able to fix! Able to provide! Able to lift! Able to give! Great is my reward! Great is my reward! Great is my reward!

I believe Christ will do what Christ said Christ would do. Christ said He would die and in three days He would rise! And He did! Jesus said, "You can tear this temple down in three days and it will rise again!" Christ died and in three days He rose. Christ said, "The Christ will suffer and in three days rise again." Christ suffered on that cross but in three day He rose with all power in His hand!

Believe that Christ keeps His promise!

Nothing's Too Hard for the Lord

Genesis 18:9-15 NIV

⁹"Where is your wife Sarah?" they asked him. "There, in the tent," he said.
¹⁰ Then the LORD said, "I will surely return to you about this time next year, and Sarah your wife will have a son." Now Sarah was listening at the entrance to the tent, which was behind him. ¹¹Abraham and Sarah were already old and well advanced in years, and Sarah was past the age of childbearing. ¹²So Sarah laughed to herself as she thought, "After I am worn out and my master is old, will I now have this pleasure?" ¹³Then the LORD said to Abraham, "Why did Sarah laugh and say, 'Will I really have a child, now that I am old?' ¹⁴Is anything too hard for the LORD? I will return to you at the appointed time next year and Sarah will have a son." ¹⁵Sarah was afraid, so she lied and said, "I did not laugh." But he said, "Yes, you did laugh."

Is anything too hard for God? Is there anything that God cannot do? Have you ever thought that something just could not be done? Have you ever thought that something was impossible, hopeless, would not change?

Barbara Folsom tells the story of a young preacher who was feeling insecure about what God wanted him to do in ministry. One day this young preacher was walking with an older more seasoned preacher in a garden. The young preacher shared with the older preacher his insecurity and asked the older preacher what he should do.

The older preacher walked up to a rose bush and handed the young preacher a rosebud and told him to open it without tearing off any of the petals.

The young preacher looked in disbelief at the older preacher and was trying to figure out what the rosebud had to do with his wanting to know the will of God for his ministry and his life. Yet, he respected the old preacher and he proceeded to try to unfold the rose while keeping the petal intact. It did not take the young preacher long to realize that it was impossible for him to do.

The old preacher noticed that the young preacher was unable to unfold the rosebud while keeping it intact, so the old preacher began telling him a poem. The poem went like this:

> It's only a tiny rosebud
> A flower of God's design;
> But I cannot unfold the petals
> With these clumsy hands of mine.
> The secret of unfolding flowers
> Is not to such as I.
> God opens this flower so sweetly,
> When in my hands they fade and die.
> If I cannot unfold a rosebud,

This flower of God's design,
Then how can I think I have wisdom
To unfold this life of mine.
So I will trust in him for his leading
Each moment of every day.
I will look to him for guidance
Each step of the pilgrim way.
The pathway that lies before me,
Only my Heavenly Father knows.
I'll trust Him to unfold the moments,
Just as He unfolds the rose.

Can you identify with this young preacher? I can, and I'm sure that you can as well. Not knowing what the future holds can be a little unsettling for most of us. We want to be in control of our future. But the reality is that we are not in control, and if we think we are we are not going very far. God controls our future, and we must trust God to lead us in the moments when we think things are impossible.

Is anything to hard for God? This is a question to which our lives revolve. This is also a question that every human being has to answer. Is God able to do what I need God to do? Is what I'm going through too difficult for God?

This is a question that is quintessential to our faith. If we answer, "Yes, what I'm going through is too hard for God," then we do not confess God as God. If we answer, "No, nothing is too hard for God" then this answer places trust in God. Not only does it place trust in God, but it also gives God the freedom to do what only God can do.

Is anything too hard for the Lord? The answer is not always as clear-cut as you might think. Is anything too hard for the Lord? We many answer, "no" with our mouths but our real answer to the question does not lie in what we say openly; the real answer lies in what we say inwardly. Our inward response to the question of whether or not we think that things are too hard for God is what God observes.

We can say one thing and then inwardly think something else. What we think inwardly only God knows. Yet, we have to deal with these inward responses.

Is there anything impossible for God? No, everything is possible for God. Nothing is too difficult for God. There is nothing that God cannot do. But do we really believe this inwardly? This is a question that we all have to deal with.

Sarai is dealing with this question in our text today. The Word of the Lord has come to Abram. The Lord said, "Eliezer of Damascus will not be your heir, but a son coming from your own body will be your heir." (Genesis 15:4) The Lord takes Abram outside and says, "Look up at the heavens and count the stars—if indeed you can count them. So shall your offspring be." (Genesis 15:5) The writer says, "Abram believed the Lord, and he credited it to him as righteous." (15:6)

Abram believes, but the writer says nothing of Sarai's belief. Sarai is still barren. She still has no children.

Sarai wants Abram to have an heir, so she tells him to sleep with her maidservant, Hagar, and perhaps, she says, Abram can build a family through her. Abram does and Hagar conceives and gives birth to Ishmael. Sarai despises Hagar. Abram is eighty-six years old when Hagar gives birth.

Hagar runs away, but the angel of the Lord tells her to go back and to submit to Sarai. When Abram is ninety-nine years old, the Lord appears to him. The Lord changes Abram's name to Abraham, and the Lord tells Abraham that he will be the father of many nations. He will be fruitful and kings will come from him. This is God's covenant to him.

As a sign of the covenant, God says, all males in Abraham's

household, Abraham's offspring or not, are to be circumcised when they is eight days old. This must be done in future generations as a sign of the covenant that God has made with Abraham.

God then tells Abraham that Sarai's name will no longer be Sarai but Sarah. The Lord says, "I will bless her so that she will be the mother of nations; kings of people will come from her."

Abraham fell to the ground laughing, saying, "Will a son be born to a man a hundred years old? Will Sarah bear a child at the age of ninety?" Abraham has another crisis of faith. Abraham says, "If only Ishmael might live under your blessing!"

The Lord says, "Yes, but your wife Sarah will bear you a son, and you will call him Isaac." The Lord tells Abraham that he will bless Ishmael and make him fruitful and will greatly increase his numbers, but Sarah will bear him a son next year.

Abraham circumcises Ishmael at thirteen, himself at ninety-nine years old and every male in his household, including those born in it and brought from a foreigner.

The Lord appears to Abraham near the great trees of Mamre. It is in the heat of the day, and Abraham is sitting at the entrance of his tent when he looks up and sees three men standing nearby. These three men appear suddenly, but it is the Lord appearing to him.

When he sees them, he hurried from his tent to meet them, and he bowed low to the ground. Abraham says, "If I have found favor in your eyes, my lord, do not pass your servant by." They are passing by his tent so he wants to show them hospitality. Abraham says, "Let a little water be brought, and then you may all wash your feet and rest under this tree. Let me get you something to eat, so you can be refreshed and then go on your way—now that you have come to your servant."

They answered, "Very well, do as you say." They rest and recline themselves as Abraham and Sarah prepare the meal.

Sarah hastily bakes cakes of bread. Abraham's servant prepares a tender calf that he has selected. He brought them milk of two forms, and he sets all of this before them.

While they ate, Abraham stands near them under the tree.

It is here that a conversation between Abraham and God takes place. It is a conversation about the power of having faith in God.

First, Abraham's and Sarah's barrenness is shattered by a new realm of possibility that is outside the reasonable expectation of their perceptual field. These three men asked, "Where is your wife Sarah?" Abraham said, "There, in the tent." The Lord said, "I will surely return to you about this time next year, and Sarah your wife will have a son."

These men ask a casual question that leads to an announcement, which basically fills the great blank that Abraham has in his life. The Lord responds to Abraham in a definite way.

Sarah is barren. She cannot have any children. Abraham is well aware of this. However, Sarah's barrenness is shattered when the Lord says to Abraham, "I will surely return to you about this time next year, and Sarah your wife will have a son."

The Lord has told Abraham this before. He still has doubts because the present has not changed. Sarah is still without a child. Yet, this is the first time the Lord is specific. The Lord says, "I will surely return to you about this time next year, and Sarah your wife will have a son."

This is outside their reasonable expectation. The text tells us so. Sarah was listening at the entrance to the tent, which was behind Abraham.

The writer says that both Abraham and Sarah were already old and well advanced in years, and Sarah was past the age of childbearing. When Sarah hears the Lord say, "surely, I will return to you about this time next year and Sarah, your wife, will have a son," Sarah laughed to herself as she thought, "After I am worn out and my master is old, will I now have this pleasure."

Sarah thinks her days of enjoyment are gone. She thinks that since her menstrual cycle is over she cannot have children. She doubts God's prophesy. Even though she and her husband cannot see, God helps them to see by saying, "surely, this will happen."

Many of us are like Sarah and Abraham. God has made a promise to us, but some of us have become impatient because the promise has not come to fruition. We think that we should have received it by now, and since we haven't, we have taken matters into our own hands. Our faith is defective because we have received the promise but are not willing to wait on the Lord to fulfill the promise.

God has given us a promise. God has told us that God will bless us; told us what we will receive as an inheritance; told us that there will come a time when our dreams will come to fruition; told us that we will become fruitful; told us that our lives will become more productive; told us that God will send us this or that; told us that there will be a day when our crops will grow a rich harvest; told us that deliverance would take place; told us that we would be healed; told us that the impossible would happen in our lives; told us that we would be taken from one degree of grace to another; told us that we would be promoted; told us that this is just the beginning of what is going to happen; told us that our descendants would be as numerous as the stars in the sky; told us that stability would come into our lives; told us that we were secure; told us that trouble don't last always; told us that all we have to do is be patient and wait on the Lord, but we haven't believed the promise.

Why do we doubt the promise of God? It couldn't be that God is not a promise keeper! You could say that about humanity, but the fact of the matter is that God has kept every single one of God's promises.

There is no one here today who can say that God did not keep God's promise. God has blessed us. God has kept us. God has promoted us.

God has been with us. God has brought us. God has healed us. God has delivered us. God has saved us. God is a promise keeper.

The reason why some doubt the promise of God is because we are trying to see things from our limited perceptual field.

Faith tells us to see that which we cannot see with our naked eyes. We can't see faith. You can have 20/20 vision and still not see faith with the naked eye. Faith is beyond our perceptual field. Faith is not something we see. Faith is something we believe. Faith shatters the realm of possibility. Faith is that which only God can do. Faith believes in that which we cannot see. Faith is trusting God to do what only God can do. Faith believes what God has promise. Faith is having trust that God will show up. Faith is that which is outside man's expectation. Faith is God saying that the impossible will be done. Faith is crediting God as saying, "Surely, by this time next month it will come to pass."

Secondly, faith is an impossible act that must fit within the normal activities of our lives. Sarah laughs when she hears the Lord say, "I will surely return to you about this time next year, and Sarah your wife will have a son." Sarah laughed to herself as she thought, "After I am worn out and my master is old, will I now have this pleasure?"

Then the Lord said to Abraham, "Why did Sarah laugh and say, 'Will I really have a child, now that I am old? Is anything too hard for the Lord? I will return to you at the appointed time next year and Sarah will have a son."

Sarah laughs because she and Abraham are accustomed to their barrenness. They have concluded that having children is out of the plan for their lives. They have accepted their barrenness; their hopelessness as normal.

God gives them the promise, but they both do not believe that Sarah will have a child in their old age. Because they doubt, God has a question for Abraham. God says, "Abraham is there anything too hard for Me?"

Let me leave my third point here.

God knows whether we have faith or not. Sarah hears what is going on outside the tent. God asks Abraham, "Why did Sarah laugh?" She is afraid. Maybe she realized it was God that she was talking to. Sarah is afraid, so she lied and said, "I did not laugh."

But God said, "Yes, you did."

Sarah is startled by the unexpected exposure to her secret. God has revealed her innermost thoughts of unbelief. And when God reveals her laughter, she withdraws because she realizes that God is speaking.

God knows whether we have faith or not. Faith is not what we say; faith is what we believe on the inside. God knows what we believe on the inside. You can't fool God. You might be able to fool man, but you can't fool God. God knows what you are thinking on the inside. God knows if you really have faith, and God knows if you are just pretending.

I like what one commentator said. He said, when God said, "Yes, Sarah, you did laugh," this was not a rebuke from God but an acknowledgement that Sarah was justified to laugh. The commentator says, "rightfully so, did Sarah laugh." He says, "The way forward in the covenant consistently passes through poverty, abandonment, and desolation. I'm sure that that memory of the promises in the midst of this vacancy and emptiness can seem cruelly funny."

We have also laughed at the promise of God. God has made a promise, and we initially laughed and said, "Yeah, Lord, right! How is that going to happen?" The promise initially sounded ridiculous. The promise at first seemed impossible. The promise when first given seemed ludicrous.

Then God said, "Is there anything too hard for Me?"

God wants to hear Abraham's response! Sarah has laughed, and God holds Abraham responsible for her response. God says, "Abraham, respond: Is there anything too hard for me?"

Many of us are like Abraham and Sarah. God has told us that our barrenness will end, but we don't believe it. God has told us that there is hope, but we are living our lives as if there is none. We have accepted life as it is without believing the future that God has for our lives.

Thus God is saying to us: "Is there anything too hard for the Lord?" Our lives revolve around this very question. Is there anything that the Lord cannot do? The Lord is asking you this question right as I speak. The Lord is asking each and everyone one of us: "Is there anything that I cannot do?"

If we say, "No, there is nothing that God cannot do," then we answer in faith. But if we say, "I don't know if God can fix this," then we don't believe, thus rejecting the promise that God has placed in our lives. When we doubt God, we limit the possibilities of God.

Please allow me to pose the question today: "Is there anything too hard for the Lord?" Is there anything that God cannot do? Is there any problem God cannot fix? Is there any trouble God cannot solve? Is there any sickness God cannot cure? Is there any obstacle God cannot remove? Is there anything broken God cannot glue back together? Is there a heart that God cannot mend? Is there any wound God cannot bandage? Is there anything God cannot put back together? Is there anything too strange for the Lord? Is anything too hard for God?

There's nothing to hard for God! There's nothing too hard for God! There's nothing too hard for God!

Faith helps us to look beyond our limited view of the future to a consideration of God's possibilities. God is competent enough to accomplish anything. God is able to do the extraordinary, the marvelous, the wonderful, the difficult and the impossible. God is able to do that which does not make any sense. God is able to make the barren pregnant, the desolate fruitful, the hopeless happy.

Nothing is too hard for God. There is nothing God cannot do. There is no problem God cannot fix. There is not trouble God cannot solve. There is no sickness God cannot cure. There is no situation God will not respond to. There is nothing broken God cannot put back together. There is no wound God cannot bandage. There is absolutely nothing God cannot put back together again. Nothing is too hard for God.

The Lord can do anything! The impossible—God can do! The difficult—God can do! The unreasonable—God can do! The ridiculous—God can do! The wondrous—God can do! What's out of the question—God can do! What others say cannot happen—God can do! What others say cannot be achieved—God can do! What's hopeless—God can do. God can do all things but fail!

Leprosy—not too hard for the Lord! Paralysis—not too hard for the Lord! Fever—not too hard for the Lord! A furious storm—not too hard for the Lord! Demon possession—not too hard for the Lord! An issue of blood—nothing to hard for the Lord! Blindness—nothing too hard for the Lord! Blindness and muteness at the same time-—nothing too hard for the Lord! Five thousand hungry men—nothing too hard for the Lord! Walking on water—nothing too hard for the Lord! Feeding of four thousand—nothing too hard for the Lord! Seizures—nothing too hard for the Lord! A piece of money in a fish's mouth—nothing to hard for the Lord! Two blind men cured—nothing too hard for the Lord! A fig tree cursed—nothing to hard for the Lord!

Arrest—nothing to hard for the Lord! Crucifixion—nothing too hard for the Lord! Death—nothing to hard for the Lord! Resurrection—nothing, absolutely nothing, too hard for the Lord!

There is nothing that the Lord cannot do. All we have to do is be patient and wait on the Lord. "Be of good courage and wait on the Lord!"

Amen. Amen. Amen.

I'm Not Perfect

Genesis 20

¹Now Abraham moved on from there into the region of the Negev and lived between Kadesh and Shur. For a while he stayed in Gerar, ²and there Abraham said of his wife Sarah, "She is my sister." Then Abimelech king of Gerar sent for Sarah and took her. ³But God came to Abimelech in a dream one night and said to him, "You are as good as dead because of the woman you have taken; she is a married woman." ⁴Now Abimelech had not gone near her, so he said, "Lord, will you destroy an innocent nation? ⁵Did he not say to me, 'She is my sister,' and didn't she also say, 'He is my brother'? I have done this with a clear conscience and clean hands." ⁶Then God said to him in the dream, "Yes, I know you did this with a clear conscience, and so I have kept you from sinning against me. That is why I did not let you touch her. ⁷Now return the man's wife, for he is a prophet, and he will pray for you and you will live. But if you do not return her, you may be sure that you and all yours will die." ⁸Early the next morning Abimelech summoned all his officials, and when he told them all that had happened, they were very much afraid. ⁹Then Abimelech called Abraham in and said, "What have you done to us? How have I wronged you that you have brought such great guilt upon me and my kingdom? You have done things to me that should not be done." ¹⁰And Abimelech asked Abraham, "What was your reason for doing this?" ¹¹Abraham replied, "I said to myself, 'There is surely no fear of God in this place, and they will kill me because of my wife.' ¹²Besides, she really is my sister, the daughter of my father though not of my mother; and she became my wife. ¹³And when God had me wander from my father's household, I said to her, 'This is how you can show your love to me: Everywhere we go, say of me, "He is my brother."' ¹⁴Then Abimelech brought sheep and cattle and male and female slaves and gave them to Abraham, and he returned Sarah his wife to him. ¹⁵And Abimelech said, "My land is before you; live wherever you like." ¹⁶To Sarah he said, "I am giving your brother a thousand shekels of silver. This is to cover the offense against you before all who are with you; you are completely vindicated." ¹⁷Then Abraham prayed to God, and God healed Abimelech, his wife and his slave girls so they could have children again, ¹⁸for the LORD had closed up every womb in Abimelech's household because of Abraham's wife Sarah.

The African-American church and one of our most prominent Pastors has been in the News much lately. In my personal opinion, this tragic situation should not be played out in the news media or in the court of public opinion. As a Pastor and as a strong advocate of the Black church, I believe that this issue should be settled between the Pastor, the accusers, and that particular church.

I credit the Pastor for speaking to his church first and then to the news media. I stand not to give my personal opinion because this is not what this moment of preachment should be about. I stand to take the ancient text and apply it to humanities predicament. I will admit that modern-day situations do often aid the Preacher in this task.

However, one statement from him to his congregation summarizes the sin of humanity. This statement does not indicate his guilt but it does again summarize the predicament of humanity. I quote: "I want you to know, as I said earlier, that I am not a perfect man. But this thing, I'm going to fight." Let me again say that I am not attempting to dissect his statement. I want to suggest to you that this is a powerful statement that puts into perspective the predicament we all face. Let's forget, if we can, the allegations that led to this statement. Instead, let us simply focus on the words: "I want you to know, as I said earlier, that I am not a perfect man. But this thing, I'm going to fight."

The reality is that none of us is perfect. None of us is righteous. Jesus said, "None is righteous but the Father in Heaven."

This means that all of us are fighting with some aspect of sin in our lives. Some sins are easy to overcome. Some sins we can repent of and just move on. Yet, there are individual sins in all of our lives that, more often than not, are not easy to overcome. They have a hold on us. They grip us. They consume us. It is so good to us that we can't let go. It has such a grip that we cannot shake it. As soon as we think that we have overcome it, it consumes us like never before.

We are not perfect men or women, boys or girls. All of us are attempting to fight some area of sin in our lives.

Even the great men of our faith committed sin. One is Abraham, the father of our faith. Abraham's sin was that he lied to Abimelech concerning Sarah being his wife just so that he, Abraham, could be given safety. God and Abimelech catch Abraham in a bald face lie.

The setting of our text for today is Gerar. Abraham has sojourned in the city-state of Gerar, the southwestern corner of Canaan, in what became Philistine territory. Abimelech is king of Gerar. There Abraham said of his wife, Sarah, "She is my sister." Sarah was a very beautiful woman, and we can conclude that Abimelech saw her as beautiful as well and took Sarah as his wife.

God came to Abimelech in a dream and said, "You are as good as dead because of the woman you have taken; she is a married woman."

A son has been promised to Abraham and Sarah. The child must be Abraham's and not from the seed of a foreign king. The narrator of the text makes it clear that Abimelech had not gone near her, so he says, "Lord, will you destroy an innocent nation? Did he not say to me, 'She is my sister,' and didn't she also say, 'He is my brother'? I have done this with a clear conscience and clean hands."

The Lord said to Abimelech in a dream, "Yes, I know you did this with a clear conscience, and so I have kept you from sinning against me. That is why I did not let you touch her. Now return the man's wife, for he is a prophet, and he will pray for you and you will live. But if you do not return her, you may be sure that you and all yours will die."

Abimelech is accused by God, gives his defense before God, and is found innocent by God.

If Abimelech keeps her, he will deserve God's punishment because he will be interfering with God's promise. The narrator says, "Early the next morning Abimelech summoned all his officials, and when he told them all that had happened, they were very much afraid."

It is here that Abimelech summons Abraham, and Abraham, the prophet of God, the father of our faith, beings to speak of his sin. Abraham's sin tells us much about my sins and your sins, and the sins of humanity.

First, sin is humanities condition. Abimelech called Abraham in and said, "What have you done to us? How have I wrong you that you have done such a great guilt upon me and my kingdom? You have done things to me that should not be done." Abimelech asked Abraham, "What was your reason for doing this?"

This is a serious sin. Before God let's a foreigner enter into Sarah God will wipe the foreigner out. His death will be by a malady, which right now prevents him from conceiving. God will not only wipe him out but his entire nation as is well. God is about to destroy the entire Philistine territory unless Abimelech speaks and pleads with God, letting God know that he is an innocent man. Abraham's lie almost had this man and his people killed. Again, God would not allow the seed to come from a foreign king. God is so serious about this that he does not let Abimelech touch Sarah.

This lets us know that sometimes we reap the benefits of others without even knowing it.

God listens and pronounces him innocent.

Abimelech summons Abraham and asked, "What have you done? Why did you do this? Why didn't you tell me the truth?

Abraham replied, "I said to myself, 'There is surely no fear of God in this place, and they will kill me because of my wife.' Besides, she really is my sister, the daughter of my father though not of my mother; and she became my wife. (During this time in ancient Israel, it was ok if a man married his half-sister on his father's side, but prohibited by Moses later on). And when God had me wander from my father's household, I said to her, 'This is how you can show your love to me: Everywhere we go, say of me, 'He is my brother.'"

Not only does Abraham put Abimelech and his whole nation in jeopardy when he lies. But he puts Sarah in jeopardy as well. Abraham deliberately betrays Sarah. She submits to him and agrees with him, but he places her life and wellbeing in jeopardy as well.

He sins by lying. His sin is also a lack of faith. Abraham does not believe the promise, which includes a son from Sarah. Furthermore, his sin is selfishness. If he believed the promise, he would not put Sarah in a situation that was simply done to keep him alive. He would have stood on the promise of God, believing that God would provide.

Abraham sinned. Some may be saying, "No, not Abraham. He is a prophet. Prophets don't sin. They don't lie. Plus, the writer of Hebrews declares, 'He is the author and finisher of our faith.'" Abraham did sin, and he did lie.

This sin predicament did not begin just today. It has been going on since the creation of the world. Sin started with Adam and Eve, and sin is our predicament today. If someone says, "I don't sin, they just did." The Bible says, "All have sinned and come far short of the glory of God." Are any of us greater than Abraham? Sin is our condition.

None of us are without sin. This includes me, as Pastor. We have to be careful how we elevate the Pastors and prophets of today. We have to be careful how we elevate those we see preaching on television. We have to be careful how we elevate our Pastors and Preachers. The Pastor, the Preacher and the prophet sins just like you do. His sin might not be your sin, and your sin might not be her sin. There is no greater degree of sin. Sin is sin. So many times we elevate the preacher, and then when the preacher's weaknesses are exposed, we are hurt. Why are you hurt? Why are you surprised? The church leader deals with some of the same stuff that those in the pew deal with. Some folk elevate the Pastor above the Christ. You ought not to elevate the Pastor-Preacher. You need to elevate the Christ that you see in him or her. "All have sinned and come far short of the glory of God."

This includes every minister sitting to my left and to my right. This includes every Deacon who is sitting in from of me. This includes everyone who is sitting in the sanctuary today. We are not perfect. We are not righteous. We are not faultless. Some of us might think we are, but we are not. "All have sinned and come far short of the glory of God." Not some, but "All." Not a few, but "All." Not a small number, but "All."

The reason why we are here today is because we are battling some stuff we need God to help us to get rid of. "All have sinned and come far short of the glory of God."

Furthermore, sin suggests that we have not learned from previous experiences. This is not the first time that Abraham lied or betrayed Sarah. Abraham lied before under the same condition.

In Chapter 12, the same thing happened. There was a famine in Canaan, and Abram and Sarai went down to Egypt to live there for a while to escape the famine. As he was about to enter into Egypt, Abram said to Sarai, "I know what a beautiful woman you are. When the Egyptians see you, they will say, 'This is his wife.' Then they will kill me but will let you live. Say you are my sister, so that I will be treated well for your sake and my life will be spared because of you."

When Abram came to Egypt, the Egyptians saw that Sarai was a very beautiful woman. When Pharaoh's officials saw her, they praised her to Pharaoh and she was taken to his palace.

He treated Abram well because of her. Abram acquired sheep and cattle, male and female donkeys, menservants and maidservants, and camels.

But the Lord knew that it was through Sarai that the promise would be given, so the Lord inflicted serious diseases on Pharaoh and his household because of Abram's wife, Sarai. Pharaoh summoned Abram and said, "What have you done to me? Why didn't you tell me she was your wife? Why did you say, 'She is my sister,' so that I took her to be my wife? Now then, here is your wife. Take her and go!"

Then Pharaoh gave orders about Abram to his men, and they sent him on his way, with his wife and everything he had.

Abram gave his wife to a Pharaoh just so he could stay alive. The text does not say whether Pharaoh slept with her or not. Yet, God got him through that and blessed him as well. And now we see Abraham doing the very same thing again. What type of man would give his wife to another man just so that he could stay alive? What type of man would not believe the promise of God, thus giving his wife to become the wife of another king? Abraham, the prophet.

Yet, this time is a greater sin because God has told him that his heir will come through his and Sarah's seed.

Let's not beat upon on Abraham, the prophet, too badly, because we have been in situations where God brought us out of a sinful situation, and after we were out of it for a while we went back and did the very same thing. We ask for forgiveness, but we went back and did it again. The Lord got us out of it one time and we went back and did it again. The Lord delivered us from it, but we went back and did it again. The Lord took the taste away, but we went back and did it again. The Lord saved our lives, but we went back and did it again. The Lord told us to leave it alone, and we went back and did it again. The Lord told us not to touch it, but we went back and touched it again. The Lord told us not to go back, but we went back again and again and again.

All of us are like Abraham. We sinned. The Lord got us out of it, and when the situation presented itself, we went back and we did it again.

Yet, I thank God that God just doesn't forgive us one time. I thank God that God doesn't forgive us two times. I thank God that God doesn't forgive us three or four times. But the Lord forgives us over and over and over again. "Jesus is faithful and just to forgive us of all of our sins and to cleanse us from all of our unrighteousness."

Thirdly, despite our sins, God still blesses us.

It is interesting here that Abraham, the father of faith, is not the one who demonstrates faith. The one who demonstrates faith is Abimelech. Abimelech believes Abraham's weak defense. Abraham does not deny his guilt. Instead, he becomes very defensive (like we do) and tries to justify his actions (like we do).

He determines that there was no fear of God in Gerar. He tries to justify his actions by saying Sarah really is his sister. He blames his situation on God (like we do as well). It was God who made him a wanderer. We see Abraham's lack of faith once again.

Abimelech could have killed Abraham because Abraham almost got him killed. But the word of God keeps Abraham alive. God has told Abimelech something that will keep Abraham alive. God says, "He is a prophet. If you return his wife, he will pray for you and you will live."

Look at what Abimelech does. Abimelech gives reparation to Abraham. By law, Abimelech had to pay compensation and damages. He had to pay a reimbursement, which was the price of a wife's compensation for injury, even though he did not touch her. He brought sheep and cattle and male and female slaves and gives them to Abraham. He even gives Abraham land. Abimelech says, "My land is before you; live wherever you like." He does not just give Abraham land. He tells Abraham to choose to live wherever he wants to live.

He even gives compensation to Abraham as Sarah's brother. He tells Sarah, "I am giving your brother a thousand shekels of silver. This is to cover the offense against you before all who are with you; you are completely vindicated." Compensation was due because of injured feelings—to the husband if the woman was married or engaged, to her relatives if she was unmarried. Therefore, he restores Sarah's honor. This is a public demonstration that she has not been wronged and hence can be held in honor within her community.

Abraham lied and almost had Abimelech and his nation wiped out, yet this man who has more fear of God than Abraham blesses the same man who almost had him killed.

Despite his sin, God still allows Abraham to be blessed.

You know where I'm going with this! God does the same for us! Despite our sin, God still blesses us. You do know that we have what we have and we are where we are simply because God has blessed us! We are not where we are because we have been so good. We don't have what we have because we have dotted every "I" and crossed every "T." We are where we are and have what we have because God blesses us despite our mess! Despite our sins, God still blesses us! Despite our faults, God still blesses us! Despite our shortcomings, God still blesses us! Despite our failings, God still blesses us! Despite our errors, God still blesses us! Despite our behaviors, God still blesses us! Despite our transgressions, God still blesses us! Despite our weaknesses, God still blesses us! Despite our inadequacies, God still blesses us! Despite our deficiencies, God still blesses us! Despite our ways, God still blesses us! Despite our thoughts, God still blesses us! Despite our offenses, God still blesses us!

Blesses us with life! Blesses us with health and strength! Blesses us with shelter! Blesses us with food! Blesses us with clothing! Blesses us with a job! Blesses us with family! Blesses us with a church! Blesses us with a little money! Blesses us with 401(k)s and IRAs! Despite our sins. Despite the mess in our lives, God keeps on blessing us over and over and over again.

Lastly, despite our sins, God still decides to use us. After Abimelech gives compensation to Abraham and Sarah, the narrator says, "Then Abraham prayed to God, and God healed Abimelech, his wife and his slave girls so they could have children again, for the Lord had closed up every womb in Abimelech's household because of Abraham's wife Sarah."

God tells Abimelech, "Return the man's wife, for he is a prophet, and he will pray for you and you will live. But if you do not return her, you may be sure that you and all yours will die."

As stated earlier, the Lord had inflicted Abimelech with a malady that made him sterile and would cause him death if he does not let Sarah go. Not only does God give him a sickness, but also all the females in his household are barren, wombs closed up by God. If he lets Sarah go, Abraham, the man who lied, the man who is struggling with his faith, the prophet, will be the one who will pray for him, and he and his will live.

Abraham prays to God. God heals Abimelech, his wife, and his slave girls so that they could have children again.

The Lord does for Abimelech the same thing that the Lord will do for Abraham. God will open up the womb of Sarah, and God will open up the womb of Abimelech's wife and slave girls. All will have children.

The text does not provide us with examples that this did happen for Abimelech's household. The text does not tell us whether or not his household had children again. But our faith tells us. Our faith tells us that God keeps God's promise. That God keeps God's Word. That God does exactly what God says that God will do. Our faith says, "Yes, Abimelech was healed! Yes, his wife had more children! Yes, his slave girls did have children again is well." We believe that it did happen because we understand that God can do all things but fail. "We walk by faith and not by sight."

71

God uses Abraham despite his sin. Abraham has been a curse, but God uses him to be a blessing. Abimelech displays faith when Abraham doesn't, but God decides to use Abraham. Despite Abraham's sin, God uses him to be the vehicle in which the entire nation is saved. Despite Abraham's sin, Abraham is still God's preferred. Despite Abraham's sin, Israel is still dependant on him. Despite Abraham's sin, the promise will still be conceive through him. Despite Abraham's sin, he will be the father of many nations. Despite Abraham's sin, God still uses him.

His words are lacking. His faith is insufficient. But because of God's grace, God still decides to use him.

John Calvin called it, "The infirmity of man and the grace of God." We sin, but because of God's grace, God continues to use us. We fall short, but God still uses us. We sin, but God still uses us. We are disobedient, but God still uses us. That which we want to do, we don't do; and that which we don't want to do, we do, but God still uses us.

Morally deficient as we are, God still uses us. Unworthy as we are, God has chosen us to be the means in which God's Gospel is proclaimed.

Thank God for using me! I'm not worthy to stand before you every Sunday, proclaiming the Word of God, but God still uses me. God uses me, and God uses you.

Despite what you have done, God still can use you. Despite your situation, God can still use you. Despite your sins, God can still use you. Despite what you did twenty years ago, God can still use you. Despite what you did on yesterday, God can still use you. Despite what your criminal record is, God can still use you. Despite what you are struggling with, God can still use you.

God can use anybody.

Why? Because Jesus paid it all. Christ came for us! Christ died for us! Christ was buried for us! Christ was resurrected for us!

"What can wash away my sin? Nothing but the blood of Jesus; What can make we whole again? Nothing but the blood of Jesus. Oh! precious is the flow that makes me white as snow; No other fount I know, Nothing but the blood of Jesus."

Who would have thought it?

Genesis 21:1-7

¹Now the LORD was gracious to Sarah as he had said, and the LORD did for Sarah what he had promised. ²Sarah became pregnant and bore a son to Abraham in his old age, at the very time God had promised him. ³Abraham gave the name Isaac to the son Sarah bore him. ⁴When his son Isaac was eight days old, Abraham circumcised him, as God commanded him. ⁵Abraham was a hundred years old when his son Isaac was born to him. Sarah said, "God has brought me laughter, and everyone who hears about this will laugh with me." ⁷And she added, "Who would have said to Abraham that Sarah would nurse children? Yet I have borne him a son in his old age."

A couple of weeks ago, I was eating breakfast in Waffle House in Fredericksburg when a gentleman got up and began asking as he pointed, "Whose black Hyundai is that?" I said to myself, "It's my car! Why in the world is he asking everyone, 'Whose car is that?'" When he got to me, he said, "Is that your black Hyundai?" I said, "Yes, sir, it is! Why do you ask?" He said, "There's an article in today's paper that says that your car model is being recalled because of steering wheel problems." He showed me the article, and I said, "Yes, sir, that's me." I thanked him and I told him that I would call the dealer right away because this was nothing to play with.

I called my buddy who is the manager of College Park Hyundai, and he said, "Man, we're having problems with the steering wheel separating from the column. You better bring it in right away, and we will straighten you out." I said, "I'll bring it in around 2:00 p.m. tomorrow." I really did not want to take it back to the dealer because I had taken it back two times, both times to reset the computer, and I had to wait about two hours each time. As you know, I'm not a patient person, and I don't like waiting at all.

Yet, I knew that driving the car was a hazard, so I decided to take it in. When I got to the dealer, they were waiting for me. I said to the service person, "Sir, how long do I have to wait? I don't have three hours." He said, "Mr. Dalton, it will take about two hours; that's if there's nothing wrong. We will take care of you. I promise to get you out as soon as I can." I said, "Thanks!"

The previous time I went, I got on their nerves, as well as they mine, because I kept on asking, "When will my car be ready?" They had no idea because they had to call headquarters to talk to them about how to reset a code on the car.

So to deal with my impatience, I walked to the shopping center, had lunch and walked around Home Depot. After I got bored with that, I walked back to the dealership and asked about my car.

The service department rep said, "Mr. Dalton, your car is ready. We placed a bolt in the steering column and you are good to go. By the way, you needed an oil and filter change so we changed your oil and replaced your filter." I said, "How much does it cost?" He said, "Nothing, this one is on us." I said, "Thank you!" He said, "I promised to take care of you." I said, "That you did!"

Some things in life are worth waiting for! In my case, the blessing of a free oil change was received. Not only are some things in life worth waiting for, but also sometimes we have to wait for promises to come to fruition. I believed the service rep when he said, "Mr. Dalton, we're going to take care of you," but I didn't know that he would keep his promise by giving me a free oil change. His promise far exceeded what I thought.

God is the same way. God keeps God's promise. God does exactly what God says that God will do. And God does what God says that God will do at the exact time God said God would do it. The problem with us is that we are unwilling to wait. We are unwilling to wait for God's promise to come to completion.

We have a hard time waiting. Society teaches us not to wait, but to take matters into our own hands. We live in a microwave ear, an era where we just want to pop everything into a microwave and then in a matter of minutes have a full-course meal. Nevertheless, a microwave meal never tastes as good as a home-cooked meal.

Some things in life are worth waiting for. Waiting on the promise of God is one thing that is worth waiting for.

God does not complete God's promise toward us overnight. Sometimes we have to wait years and years for God's promise to come true in our lives. Yet, the reality is that God keeps every promise that God makes to us.

Our text for today teaches us this. I like the way the narrator begins our text. The narrator says, "Now the Lord was gracious to Sarah as he had said, and the Lord did for Sarah what he had promised."

The Lord promised Sarah that she would give birth to a son. The Lord told Abraham in Chapter 18, "I will surely return to you about this time next year, and Sarah your wife will have a son."

Sarah, who was listening, laughed to herself and thought, "After I am worn out and my master is old, will I now have this pleasure?" Abraham and Sarah are old and Sarah is well past the childbearing age.

The Lord says to Abraham, "Why did Sarah laugh and say, 'Will I really have a child now that I am old?' Is anything too hard for the Lord? I will return to you at the appointed time next year and Sarah will have a son."

Sarah does become pregnant as the Lord has said, and she gives birth to a son at the time God has promised Abraham.

Abraham named this son Isaac, which means, "He laughs." When Isaac was eight days old, Abraham circumcised him as God commanded him. Abraham was one hundred years old and Sarah ninety when Isaac was born.

Sarah says, "God has brought me laughter, and everyone who hears about this will laugh with me." She added, "Who would have said to Abraham that Sarah would nurse children? Yet I have borne him a son in his old age."

This text reminds us much about God.

It tells us that God does what God says that God will do. God does it when God promises God will do it. And when God does it, God does it in such a way that we laugh in amazement.

First, the text teaches us that God makes good on God's promises. God in Chapter 17 (verses 15-21) has told Abraham that God will bless Sarah and she will surely give him a son. God tells Abraham that he will "bless her so that she will be the mother of nations; kings of peoples will come from her."

Abraham falls facedown, laughs, and says to himself, "Will a son be born to a man a hundred years old? Will Sarah bear a child at the age of ninety?" Abraham says to God, "If only Ishmael might live under your blessing!"

God said, "Yes, but your wife Sarah will bear you a son, and you will call him Isaac. I will establish my covenant with him as an everlasting covenant for his descendants after him. And as for Ishmael, I have heard you: I will surely bless him; I will make him fruitful and greatly increase his numbers. He will be the father of twelve rulers, and I will make him into a great nation. But my covenant I will establish with Isaac, whom Sarah will bear to you by this time next year."

Now in Chapter 21, the writer says in verses 1-2, "Now the Lord was gracious to Sarah as he had said, and the Lord did for Sarah what he had promised. Sarah became pregnant and bore a son to Abraham in his old age, at the very time God had promised him."

The birth of Isaac is promised. The time of his birth is given. "This time next year Sarah will give you a son." And God keeps God's promise. Sarah gives birth to Isaac. The Lord is gracious to her. The Lord did for her exactly what the Lord had promised and the Lord did it exactly when the Lord said the Lord would do it.

God is a promise keeper. God does exactly what God said God would do. Has God ever promised you something and then reneged on God's promise? Has God ever made a promise that God did not keep? Has God ever told you something that you later found out was a lie? Has God ever told you something that did not come to pass? Has God ever assured you of something and that which God assured did not happen? Has God ever told you that God was going to do something that God did not do?

The answer to all the above is, "No!" Why? Because God is a promise keeper. God does what God says God was going to do; when God said God was going to do it; how God said God was going to do it, why God said God was going to do it, and where God says God was going to do it.

God is a promise keep. God keeps every promise. God answers every prayer. God gives us a solution to every promise. God makes a way out of no way. God performs miracles with wonders to perform. God makes good on every promise that God makes. When God says something, you can take God to the bank. God is a promise keeper.

Secondly, God gets involved in some way when the roads into the future seem blocked. Sarah becomes pregnant and gives Abraham a son in his old age. The writer says in verse 5, "Abraham was a hundred years old when his son Isaac was born to him." Sarah is ninety and Abraham is one hundred when Isaac is born.

Some twenty-five years have passed since God told Abraham to leave his country, his people, and his father's household for a land that God will show him. Twenty-five years have passed since God first told Abraham, "I will make you into a great nation and I will bless you; I will make your name great, and you will be a blessing. I will bless those who bless you, and whoever curses you I will curse; and all peoples on earth will be blessed through you."

Twenty-five years have passed, and now, finally, the promise has come to fruition. The road seemed blocked for Abraham and Sarah. Sarah's age of childbearing has come and gone. Her womb is closed. Her menstrual cycle is over. Hagar has given birth to Ishmael. She is ninety years old. Abraham is one hundred. Yet, God has declared, "Nothing is too hard for the Lord."

God opened every door that Abraham and Sarah thought was closed. God removed every obstacle that Abraham and Sarah thought would prevent them from having a son. They thought that they were as good as dead, but God opened the door they thought were closed. They had lost hope, but God turned their hopelessness into joy.

I'm sure today that all of us, if not most of us, are waiting on a promise from the Lord. Abraham and Sarah waited twenty-five years. Some in here may have been waiting longer than that.

You have been waiting, but all you see is roadblock after roadblock, obstacle after obstacle, detour after detour, rejection after rejection, bad news after bad news, barrier after barrier, impediment after impediment, problem after problem, hurdle after hurdle and hindrance after hindrance.

You do not see how the future that God has promised will come to pass. The future seems to be at an impasse. There is Good News! The Good News is that God always gets involved in some way or another when the road into your future seems blocked.

The Lord has promised us, and we, like the Psalmist, have been praying, "Lord, how long?" "Lord, how much longer do I have to wait? Will it ever come to pass? Will the anguish ever end? Lord, how much longer do I have to wait?"

It is when things seem to be at a standstill that God, in some way or another, gets involved. And when God gets involved, things begin to happen. When God gets involved, predicaments start to change. When God gets involved, the sun begins to shine.

God begins to move when our future seems to be at a standstill. God removes roadblocks. God knocks down obstacles. God gets rid of detours. God turns rejection into reception and bad news into good news. God does away with barriers. God destroys impediments. God solves problems. God allows you to leap over hurdles. God takes away the hindrances that may be.

Why? Because God wants you to receive what God has promised. God wants your future to be blessed. God wants your bareness to turn into fertility. And in order to do that, God has to get involved. When God gets involved, God removes anything that might keep the promise, your future, from becoming reality.

Next, the fulfillment of God's promise always brings us joy. Abraham names the child Isaac, which means, "He laughs." Sarah says, "God has brought me laughter, and everyone who hears about this will laugh with me."

God has kept God's promise to Sarah. God has kept God's promise by opening the door to her future. She was once barren; now she has given birth. She once did not believe, but now she believes. She is old, but despite her age, God still provides. Sarah finds God to be faithful, and thus Sarah laughs. She was once embarrassed because she did not have a child, but now her embarrassment has turned into laughter. Sarah was once in anguish, but now she laughs. God's graciousness and God's promise cause Sarah to laugh.

By God's powerful word, God has broken the grip of death, hopelessness and barrenness.

God is the giver of laughter. That's God's gift to us. God gave us the gift of laughter. Sarah can now laugh because God has proven to her that "nothing is too hard for the Lord."

Don't let anyone fool you! God is the source of our joy. The problem with the world today is that we are looking for joy/happiness in all the wrong places. True laughter and joy can come only from God. True joy will not come in the form of a man or a woman, a husband or a wife. True happiness will not come in the form of a five-bedroom house with a two-car garage. True happiness will not come in the form of a luxury vehicle. True happiness will not come in the form of a big portfolio with stock, bonds, and CDs. These things will come and go. They will rot and decay. They will be here one moment and gone the next.

But real joy comes from the Lord, and God's joy doesn't come and go. God's joy last forever. "The joy of the Lord is our strength."

When we realize that God has been gracious to us, we feel joy on the inside. When God fulfills God's promise in our lives, we can't help but to laugh. When God does what God has promised, we can't help but to feel good on the inside. When God does the impossible in our lives, we can't help but to share with others what the Lord has done for us.

When we receive the promise of God, our lives are forever changed. Our lives are no longer the same. When God end our bareness, all we can do is laugh and celebrate.

God is the only One who can bring joy to our hearts. Notice that I said God, not man, not woman, not money, not material things, but God. And God does it when God grants God's promises. That's why the old folk said, "This joy that I have, the world didn't give it, and the world can't take it away."

Not only does the fulfillment of God's promise cause us to laugh, but it also causes us to respond verbally in a way that essentially says, "Who would have thought this would ever happen to me?"

Sarah adds, "Who would have said to Abraham that Sarah would nurse children? Yet I have borne him a son in his old age."

Sarah says, "No one would have dreamed of announcing to Abraham that two old people would become parents." Abraham and Sarah did not believe it even though God said it.

This suggests that anyone would have doubted that this would happen.

The fulfillment of the promise of God leaves us with the same expression. "Who would have imagined that this would have happened to me?"

Take an inventory of your life. And if you would be honest with yourself, this has been your response. "Who would have thought this would ever happen to me?" "Who would have thought I would be where I am today? Who would have thought that I would be who I am today? Who would have thought that I would work where I work? Who would have thought that I would retire from where I retired from? Who would have thought that I would be preaching? Who would have thought that I would be in the church? Who would have thought that I would be married with children? Who would have thought that I would still be living? Who would have thought that I would survive that accident? Who would have thought that I would be cancer free? The doctors said that I would not live five years. Who would have thought that I would have made it through that illness? Who would have thought fifteen or twenty years later that I would still be living?"

Man had given up on me. The world thought that I wouldn't amount to anything. People had given up on me. But God kept God's promise. God knocked down barriers. Now I am where I am, and I am who I am simply because of the grace of God. Who would have thought that I would be here today? "Who would have thought this would ever happen to me?"

God specializes in things that are impossible to him or her who believes. God specializes in that which is not feasible, that which is unworkable, that which has no solution, that which is ludicrous, that which makes no sense, that which is not viable, that which is unworkable, that which is out of the question, that which is unachievable and unattainable.

God takes that which is impossible and makes it possible. God takes that which unfeasible and makes it feasible. God takes that which is unworkable and makes it workable. God takes that which has no solution and gives it a solution. God takes that which is not viable and makes it possible. God takes that which is out of the question and makes it possible. God takes that which is unachievable and makes it achievable. God takes that which is unattainable and makes it attainable.

God's promise causes us to proclaim, "Who would have thought this would have happened to me?"

God gives life where only death seems to reign. Sarah's womb was closed, but God's gives life. Sarah has no children, but God gives life. Sarah is sterile, but God makes her fertile.

Wherever there is death, God gives life. All we have to do is go to the cross. The Roman Soldiers hung Jesus high and they stretched Him wide. They pierced Jesus in His side. They mocked Jesus and they called Him all kinds of names. They said, "If you are the king of the Jews come down and save yourself." They said, "Leave Him alone. Let's see if Elijah comes to save Him."

Jesus cried out in a loud voice and gave up His sprit.

Joseph of Arimathea puts Jesus in his own new tomb that he had cut out of rock. He rolled a big stone in front of the entrance. Mary and Mary Magdalene were sitting there opposite the tomb.

They put a guard at the tomb. Death seemed to reign. The future seemed to have ended. All hope seemed to have been lost.

But early Sunday morning, these same women went to the tomb and the stone had rolled away. They went to the tomb, and the angel said, "I know that you are looking for Jesus, who was crucified. He is not here; he has risen just as He said. Come and see where He lay."

They looked and He had risen with all power in His hands.

Wherever there is death, Jesus gives life. Have I got a witness in here? Death can become life because Jesus has risen from the grave. Hopelessness can become reality because Jesus rose from the grave.

Barrenness can become conception because Jesus has risen from the grave. Weeping can turn into joy because Jesus has risen from the grave. Sorrow can turn into laughter because Jesus has risen from the grace. The impossible becomes possible because Jesus has risen from the grave.

It did happen because Jesus has risen from the grace.

God has a way of turning life into death and hopelessness into reality.

The Lord will Provide

Genesis 22:1-14

¹Some time later God tested Abraham. He said to him, "Abraham!" "Here I am," he replied. ²Then God said, "Take your son, your only son, Isaac, whom you love, and go to the region of Moriah. Sacrifice him there as a burnt offering on one of the mountains I will tell you about." ³Early the next morning Abraham got up and saddled his donkey. He took with him two of his servants and his son Isaac. When he had cut enough wood for the burnt offering, he set out for the place God had told him about. ⁴On the third day Abraham looked up and saw the place in the distance. ⁵He said to his servants, "Stay here with the donkey while I and the boy go over there. We will worship and then we will come back to you." ⁶Abraham took the wood for the burnt offering and placed it on his son Isaac, and he himself carried the fire and the knife. As the two of them went on together, ⁷Isaac spoke up and said to his father Abraham, "Father?" "Yes, my son?" Abraham replied. "The fire and wood are here," Isaac said, "but where is the lamb for the burnt offering?" ⁸Abraham answered, "God himself will provide the lamb for the burnt offering, my son." And the two of them went on together. ⁹When they reached the place God had told him about, Abraham built an altar there and arranged the wood on it. He bound his son Isaac and laid him on the altar, on top of the wood. ¹⁰Then he reached out his hand and took the knife to slay his son. ¹¹But the angel of the LORD called out to him from heaven, "Abraham! Abraham!" "Here I am," he replied. ¹²"Do not lay a hand on the boy," he said. "Do not do anything to him. Now I know that you fear God, because you have not withheld from me your son, your only son." ¹³Abraham looked up and there in a thicket he saw a ram caught by its horns. He went over and took the ram and sacrificed it as a burnt offering instead of his son. ¹⁴So Abraham called that place The LORD Will Provide. And to this day it is said, "On the mountain of the LORD it will be provided."

Today we begin to celebrate 125 years of ministry and service to God and to community. Not only do we celebrate 125 years of ministry and service to God and community, but also just as importantly we celebrate 125 years of God ministering to us as this church called Mount Moriah Baptist Church.

We praise God for those twenty-six founders who, in 1885, were led by the Holy Spirit in founding this church. In an era in which churches are closing every day, we thank God for allowing us to survive this long. In an era where churches are struggling for membership and discipleship, God is still using this church to lead souls to Christ, to demonstrate the standard of Christian living, and to spread the Gospel of Jesus Christ. I thank God for this!

I thank God for those who have gone on before us. I thank God for Scott, Dent, Randolph, Williams and Hailes for paving the way for me to succeed them. Oftentimes, I am asked to tell about Mount Moriah and I say, "I'm the sixth Pastor and 125 years." I have to say no more because six Pastors in 125 years tells what a great church God has allowed us to become.

The church has changed much in 125 years. Today's church, in many cases, operates on emotionalism and not via the direction of the Holy Spirit. We live in a consumerist and capitalistic society today, much different than 125 years ago. Biblical ignorance is at an all-time high. People don't know the Bible. Persons cannot quote scripture. People do not want to hear what God has to say. We seem to live in an age where we are struggling with the question, "What does it mean to be Christian?" America is not a melting pot anymore. We are a mosaic society. People from all over the globe constitute these United States of America, thus we are left with the question: What is the role of God in a multicultural and multi-religious world? Things are different, yet things are very much the same.

Even though we have an African-American president in office, racism hasn't changed one bit. Racism today is deeper than the "N" word. Have you ever seen so much hate for one man? Some Americans literally hate Barack. Some of you thought that we had arrived when Barack Obama become president. Oh, no! Racism is still alive and as ugly as ever.

There is an age-old question that I want to deal with today. It is a question that the text presents to us today. It is a question that is much older than 125 years. It is a question that is as old as time. There is this age-old question of "theodicy." Theodicy studies God's goodness and God's power in view of the presence of evil in the world. Theodicy asks questions such as: Why does a good God allow evil things to happen? Why does God allow bad things to happen to good people? One question I heard this past week was: Why did God allow a pastor to lose his wife, mother and two daughters in five years? Another: Why did God allow my favorite brother to die of AIDS at a young age? Why does God allow the evil to prosper and the righteous to struggle? Why did God allow 911 to happen? Why did God allow the earthquake in Haiti? Why did God allow the massive floods in India to kill so many people? Why does God allow natural disasters to occur, killing so many innocent people? Why does God allow babies to die? These are questions of theodicy.

These questions can be more personal: Why did God take my mother? Why did God stricken me with cancer? Why did I lose my job? Why am I unemployed? Why is my house in foreclosure? I was the one who got great evaluations. Those who didn't still have theirs and I not mine. Why, Lord? Why hasn't my child lived up to his or her God-given potential? Why has this happened to me? Why does a good and powerful God allow evil things to happen in the world and in our lives?

In our text for preachment today, we find God testing Abraham. God says to him, "Abraham!" Abraham responds, "Here I am." God says, "Take you son, your only son Isaac, whom you love, and go to the region of Moriah. Sacrifice him there as a burnt offering on one of the mountains I will tell you about."

Early the next morning, Abraham gets up, saddles his donkey, and takes two of his servants, his son Isaac, enough wood for a burnt offering and he sets out for the place God has told him about.

On the third day, he looks up and sees the place in the distance. Abraham tells his servants to stay with the donkey while he and Isaac go and worship. Abraham takes the wood for the burnt offering and places it on his son Isaac while Abraham himself takes the fire and the knife. As the two of them are walking together, Isaac speaks up and says to his father, Abraham, "The fire and wood are here, but where is the lamb for the burnt offering?" Abraham answered, "The Lord will provide the lamb for the burnt offering, my son." And the two of them went on together.

When both reach the place God has told them about, Abraham builds an altar there and arranges the wood on it. He bounds Isaac and places him on the altar, on top of the wood. He reaches out his hand to kill his son. All of a sudden an angel of the Lord calls out to him from heaven, "Abraham! Abraham! "Abraham replies, "Here I am."

The angel says, "Do not lay a hand on the boy. Do not do anything to him. Now I know that you fear God, because you have not withheld from me your son, your only son."

Abraham looks up and there in a thicket he sees a ram caught by his horns. He grabs it and sacrifices it as a burnt offering instead of his son. Abraham called the place, "The Lord will provide." The text says, "And to this day it is said, 'On the mountain of the Lord it will be provided.'"

Abraham dealt with this question of theodicy. There are times in our lives when we, too, must deal with the question of theodicy. When these times exist, we must remember that not only does God test us, but God also provides for us.

First, when dealing with questions of evil in this present age, we must first understand that God sends tests into our lives.

The text in verses 1-2 say, "Some time later God tested Abraham. He said to him, 'Abraham!' 'Here, I am, he replied.' Then God said, 'Take your son, your only son, Isaac, whom you love, and go to the region of Moriah. Sacrifice him there as a burnt offering on one of the mountains I will tell you about.'" God calls Abraham and Abraham responds in faith by saying, "Here I am."

God tests Abraham. Please note that God tests and the devil tempts. God allows the devil to tempt us, as God allowed the devil to do to Job, but God tests us. God's test to Abraham is for him to take his only son, the son he loves, the son he has been waiting twenty-five years for and go to the region of Moriah to sacrifice him as a burnt offering.

God wants to know whether or not Abraham is obedient to God. God's plan is not to kill Isaac but to test Abraham's faith. God knows that Abraham can pass the test, but God wants to know whether or not Abraham will. God genuinely does not know whether or not Abraham will do as God says, so God has to test him.

For Abraham, this is a difficult but not impossible test. Abraham has sent Ishmael away. Isaac is Abraham's and Sarah's only son. They have waited twenty-five years for his birth. Abraham and Sarah have bore him in their old age. Isaac has brought joy to their hearts. God has kept God's promise to them and now God wants to see if Abraham really is going to be obedient to what God says. God wants to know whether or not Abraham will withhold his only son from God. God wants to know whether or not God can trust Abraham in the future.

Abraham does trust God, because he goes and does as God commands. He takes Isaac to the land of Moriah to offer him as a sacrifice to God. Abraham leaves the situation up to God, trusting that God will resolve it and God will fix it.

God knows that Abraham can pass the test, but God wants to see whether or not Abraham will.

God also tests us. We are not exempt from the tests of God. There are times when God tests our faithfulness. There are times when God tests us to see how obedient we are going to be. There are times when God wants to know whether or not God is first and foremost in our lives. There are times in which God tests our hearts to see whether it belongs to God or to someone or something else. There are times in which God wants to know whether or not God can trust us with the future that God wants to place in our lives.

And when faced with tests, we must realize that we are able to pass them. God does not give us a test that we cannot pass. If we could not pass the test, then God would not have given it to us. God knows we can pass the test, but God wants to see whether or not we will. Tests are a part of all of our lives.

Some may be asking, "Why does God test us?" God gives us the answer in verse 16. God says to Abraham in verses 16-17, "I swear by myself that because you have done this and have not withheld your son, your only son, I will surely bless you and make your descendants as numerous as the stars in the sky and as the sand on the seashore." God will bless Abraham because he passed the test.

Every obstacle in life is just a test. If we pass the test, we receive the blessing. If someone falsely accuses you, it's nothing but a test. If your day is filled with setbacks, it's nothing but a test. If the ball is not bouncing in your court, it's nothing but a test.

God wants to bless us, but we have to pass the test. God wants to give to us, but we have to pass the test. God wants to make our lives fertile, but we have to pass the test.

So when we face tests, we must trust God to resolve the situation. When we face tests, we must trust God to fix it. When we face tests, we must believe that God has our best interest in mind. When we face the tests, God has to know that we will follow God wherever God leads us.

Tests by God are just a part of life.

Next, Christianity itself calls us to make sacrifices. This is not necessarily in relationship to the question of theodicy, but this is great for us as we celebrate 125 years of ministry and service.

The narrator says in verse 2, "God then says, 'Take your son, your only son, Isaac, whom you love, and go to the region of Moriah. Sacrifice him there as a burnt offering on one of the mountains I will tell you about.'"

Just imagine! Abraham at the age of 100 and the love of his life, Sarah, at the age of ninety have a son named Isaac. Abraham has a child named Ishmael by Sarah's servant Hagar years before. Hagar and Ishmael have been sent away. Isaac is Sarah's and Abraham's only son. He is the heir of Abraham. They love him so much. And now the Lord is telling Abraham to take his only son, the one that he loves so much to this mountain called Moriah to offer him as a sacrifice. Just imagine how Abraham must have felt! Just imagine yourself taking your only son or your daughter, the one whom you have waited years for, the one whom you love so much, and offering him or her as a sacrifice unto the Lord. It must have been difficult. Nonetheless, Abraham was willing to make this sacrifice.

We may not be required to offer our children as a sacrifice, but each and every one of us who is here today is required by God to make some sacrifices in our lives. We are required by God to make sacrifices so that God's will might be done in our lives.

That's the reason why this church is called Mount Moriah. When the twenty-six founders of this church met in 1885 in the home of Brother Sampson Thomas at 1220 Second Street, SW, they "believed that they were to be offered for service and sacrifice." Our church profile says, "In a biblical sense, the founders likened themselves to Abraham whom God tempted."

What are you willing to sacrifice to God? You don't have to respond to me. I'm not the judge. God is. Yet, this question needs to be answered. Mount Moriah, what are you willing to sacrifice? What are you willing to give up so that God can use you for God's glory? What are you willing to leave behind so that God's will might be done in your life?

What sacrifices is Mount Moriah willing to make so that this church might be a beacon to this community? What is Mount Moriah willing to do to let this community know that there is a church that cares for those around it? What sacrifices are we as a church willing to make?

What are you willing to relinquish? What are you willing to give up? What are you willing to forfeit? What are you willing to lose so that Christ might be gained?

The Lord did not let Abraham sacrifice Isaac. God turned Abraham around, and when he turned around he saw a ram caught in the bush by its horns. Abraham went and got it and offered it as a burnt offering instead of his son.

Just as God sent Abraham a ram as a sacrifice, God sent Jesus as our sacrificial lamb.

God sent God's son. God sent the one God loved. But God loved you and me I so much that God sent God's only son as a sacrificial lamb so that you and I might have life and have it more abundantly.

Jesus was our sacrificial lamb. Jesus, the Lamb of God, died to forgive us of our sins. The Lamb died so that we might live. The Lamb died so that we could rise above our shortcomings. The Lamb also rose with all power in His hands so that we might be able to deny ourselves, takes up our crosses daily and follow Him. The Lamb got up so that heaven could be our home.

We thank Jesus for being the sacrifice for our sins. And just as Christ was our sacrifice, we, too, are called to "be living sacrifices that are holy and accepted unto God which is our reasonable service."

What are you willing to sacrifice for the living Christ?

Third, theodicy demands that we exercise faith in God. Early the next morning, Abraham exercises faith in God. Abraham get s up and saddles his donkey. He takes with him two of his servants and his only son, Isaac. Abraham cuts enough wood for the burnt offering. And he sets out for the place that God has told him about.

On the third day, Abraham looks up and sees the place in the distance. I wonder what is going on in Abraham's heart. Abraham tells his servants to stay there with the donkey while he and Isaac go and worship and then they will come back.

Abraham has faith that he and his son, Isaac, will come back.

Abraham takes the wood for the burnt offering and places it on his son, Isaac. Isaac carries the heavier load while Abraham carries the more dangerous fire and knife. As they walk together, Isaac speaks up in curiosity and says to Abraham, "Father." Abraham responds, "Yes my son." Isaac said, "The fire and the wood are here, but where is the lamb for the burnt offering?" Abraham answers in an irrepressible affection of faith: "God himself will provide the lamb for the burnt offering, my son." And the two of them went on together.

We see the efficiency of Abraham. Abraham is obedient. He is willing to sacrifice his only son. He will do so without hesitation or delay. He will follow the command so much so that he loads the wood onto Isaac and takes the fire and the knife in his hand.

Not only is Abraham obedient, but also Abraham trusts God. Abraham stays on course because he trusts that God will save Isaac. He relays to Isaac what he believes will be the truth concerning his future. That trust is, "The Lord will provide."

That's Good News for us who are here today. For 125 years this church has declared, "God will provide." That's the ultimate statement of faith. "God will provide." That's the ultimate statement of trust. "God will provide."

I will be honest with you! I don't worry any more about what happens or doesn't happen in the church. I've learned that the Lord will provide. This is God's church, and God will take care of God's church. God has provided for 125 years, and God will provide for the next 125 years. "The Lord will provide."

This is the same type of faith that we must have in our personal lives. We must have the type of faith that says, "The Lord will provide." This is a statement of faith that proclaims what God will do. It's a futuristic statement: "The Lord will provide."

Somebody need to hear this today! "The Lord will provide." When you fall short, the Lord will provide. When things are not the way you want them, the Lord will provide. When there are obstacles before you, the Lord will provide. When the rain is falling, the Lord will provide. When others say it cannot be done, the Lord will provide. When things seem impossible, the Lord will provide. Despite the odds being against you, the Lord will provide.

"The Lord will provide." It sounds good just saying it. "The Lord will provide." The Lord will supply. The Lord will deliver. The Lord will contribute. The Lord will make it happen. The Lord will give. The Lord will satisfy. The Lord will meet our needs. The Lord will solve the problem. The Lord will fulfill the need. The Lord will make up for the lack. The Lord will make available. "The Lord will provide."

The theological notion of theodicy finally suggests that God does resolve the crisis. The Lord does provide.

The angel of the Lord called Abraham from heaven saying, "Abraham, Abraham!" Abraham responds, "Here I am." God calls and Abraham is obedient to the call of God.

The angel said, "Do not lay your hand on the boy or do anything to him; for now I know that you fear God, since you have not withheld your son, your only son, from me."

Abraham fears God. The emotion of fear is a positive form of faithfulness. Fear produces perfect obedience. The angel says, "I see you fear God so much that you will give your only child."

The fear of judgment produces obedience. The problem with many of us is that we don't fear God. Some of us just do whatever we want to do without realizing that judgment will come from God. There is also the fear that produces reverence and awe for the Divine. We should fear God because God is Holy and Divine. Fear itself produces obedience.

The sacrifice of Isaac has no other purpose than to test Abraham. Abraham looks up and sees a ram, caught in a thicket by its horns. God has provided a ram caught in the thickets for Abraham to sacrifice.

The text says, "Abraham went and took the ram and offered it up as a burnt offering instead of his son. So Abraham called the place 'The Lord will provide", as it is said to this day, 'On the mount of the Lord it shall be provided.'"

Abraham took the risk that God would provide.

The story begins with a test but ends with the Lord providing. Abraham believed that his son would not be the sacrifice. And because he believed, the ram did not appear by accident. It did not occur by happenstance. It did not occur out of luck. The ram was present simply because Abraham believed that the Lord would provide, and the Lord did provide.

And thus Abraham proclaimed, *Jehvoah-jireh*, which in the Hebrew means, "God will see" or "God will provide."

I like how the writer ends the narrative. The writer says, "On the mount of the Lord it shall be provided." One scholar rendered it this way, "As it is said to the day, 'On this mount one sees the Lord.'"

That's my prayer as we being this celebration. My prayer is that "On this mount people will see the Lord." That's my prayer. My prayer is that every time you enter and leave these sacred doors, you will declare, "On this mount I have seen the Lord."

After all, that's why we come. We come to see the Lord. You don't come to see the preacher. You don't come to see the choir. You don't come to see the ushers. You don't come to see your friend. You don't come to see that good-looking man or that beautiful woman, but we come to see the Lord. We come to feel the Lord's presence. We come to feel the power of the Holy Spirit. We come to experience the Lord's majesty. We come to acknowledge that God is worthy. We come to see the Lord's majesty. We came to see the Lord's power. We come to see the Lord's splendor. We come to see the Lord's magnificence. We come to see the Lord's greatness. We come to see the Lord's beauty. We come to see the Lord's glory. We come to see the Lord's brilliance. We come to see the Lord's luster. We come to see the Lord's holiness. We come to see the Lord's miracle-working power. We come to see the Lord's light. The come to worship the Lord in Spirit and in truth.

My prayer is that when we leave this place, we all will declare, "On this mount we have seen the Lord."

Jehovah-jireh—the Lord will see and the Lord provides. Abraham went from "the Lord will provide" to the "Lord provides."

When we pass the test, when we makes sacrifices, when we are obedient to God, when we trust God to provide, God will do just that. The Lord provided.

If we trust God, our proclamation of "The Lord will provide," we turn into "The Lord provides."

I don't know what you are going through today, but the Lord provides. I don't know what you will face on tomorrow, but I do know "The Lord provides." I don't know what we as a church will face in the days to come, but I do know "The Lord provides."

Thomas Dorsey put it this way: "The Lord will make a way somehow, When beneath the cross I bow, He will take away each sorrow, Let Him have your burdens now; When the load bears down so heavy. The weight is shown upon my brow. There's a sweet relief in knowing, O, the Lord will make a way somehow."